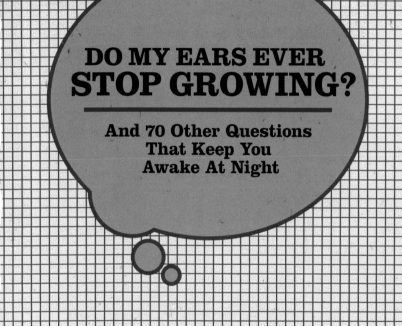

DO MY EARS EVER
STOP GROWING?

And 70 Other Questions
That Keep You
Awake At Night

© 2009 Gusto Company AS
Published exclusively for Metro Books by Gusto Company AS

Written by Michael Powell
Executive editor Gusto Company James Tavendale
Designed by Allen Boe

ISBN: 978-1-4351-1200-1

1 3 5 7 9 10 8 6 4 2

DO MY EARS EVER STOP GROWING?

And 70 Other Questions That Keep You Awake At Night

Michael Powell

METRO BOOKS
NEW YORK

CONTENTS

INTRODUCTION

An ancient Chinese proverb advises: "One who asks a question is a fool for five minutes; one who does not ask a question remains a fool forever." Questions come naturally to us, and we begin asking them as soon as we can talk: "Why is the sky blue?" "Why is it time to take a nap?" "Who lives in that tree?" Answers to the questions we ask help us to learn about our world. As we get older many of us stop viewing the world around us with innocence and wonder; we begin to focus instead on practical questions such as "How the hell am I going to pay this bill?" or "Can I get away with parking there?"

Every quest begins by asking a question. This book attempts to answer some of life's quirkier ones, big and small, from the possibility of time travel to the reason why you can't tickle yourself—things we've all asked ourselves at one time or another, but have never had the time to find out.

Some of these questions probably taxed the gray matter of our Neolithic ancestors, just as they continue to perplex us today: Do insects sleep? What is the uvula for? Why do salmon swim upstream to spawn?

Uncompromising and always entertaining, this book surveys a wide range of essential world knowledge and tackles some of the tough questions that keep you awake at night.

HOW CAN I SET UP MY OWN COUNTRY?

The short answer is "with great difficulty," but that hasn't stopped several people from trying, most recently the British comedian Danny Wallace who attempted to set up a new country in his one-bedroom flat in London's East End.

The rewards of national sovereignty are very tempting: tax exemption, becoming king or queen of your very own micronation, and diplomatic immunity for starters. But before you order a plastic crown from eBay and start printing your own currency, read on.

Since all of the land on Earth has already been claimed by existing countries, the only way that you can start a country from scratch is to discover (or create) a previously unclaimed island outside the territorial waters of other nations. However, if you don't have the means to protect the new country, it will probably be taken over by the nearest neighbor.

In 1971 a Las Vegas real estate millionaire by the name of Michael Oliver devised a cunning plan to create his own sovereign nation. The site he chose for his new project was a coral atoll called Minerva Reefs, located 260 miles southwest of the Pacific island Kingdom of Tonga. It belonged to no one because it was outside the territorial waters of all other countries and because it disappeared under water at high tide. Oliver used a dredging ship to build up the atoll until a few acres remained permanently above sea level, and then he claimed it as his own. He planned to attract investment and expand his empire by laying down yet more silt. If only Oliver's country had gained international recognition, it would have benefited from the prohibition of the use of force under the United Nations Charter. At the time, however, no such recognition existed, so when the King of Tonga sailed over with ninety men, tore down Oliver's flag, and claimed the atoll for his kingdom, Oliver's empire-building dreams quickly collapsed.

Military intervention aside, international law specifies exacting requirements for statehood. The prospective country must have a defined territory, a permanent population, and a government. The biggest hurdle is political—the country must be recognized by the international community. The size of the land doesn't matter: the Vatican is only a few square miles and the Principality of Sealand is a 10,000-square-foot oil platform in the North Sea. The 900-year-old Sovereign Order of Malta is represented by a handful of buildings in Rome, but it has diplomatic relations with 100 countries and observer status at the United Nations.

If the rest of the world doesn't take your new country seriously, then it doesn't exist in any meaningful sense. For example, Somaliland, an autonomous region in the Somali Republic in the Horn of Africa, declared its own local government in 1991, but it still is not recognized by any other country or international organization. Declaring a patch of land an independent country is rather like claiming that you are one of the most beautiful people on Earth: if the rest of the world doesn't share your opinion, then it isn't true.

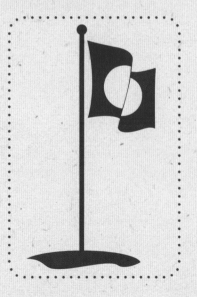

WHY IS LAUGHTER GOOD MEDICINE?

Few people would dispute that laughter feels good, but the mechanics, biochemistry, and psychological components of laughter offer genuine health benefits.

When we laugh our bodies produce natural painkillers and feel-good chemicals such as endorphins. Endorphins give us a "natural high" and ease pain. They are released when an athlete wins a race, when we have sex, or when we experience pleasure or think of things which give us pleasure. William Bloom, one of the world's leading holistic teachers, wrote a seminal book on the subject in 2001 entitled *The Endorphin Effect*, which argues that endorphins are miracle hormones that provide the foundation for good health, well-being, and elevated states of consciousness. Put quite simply, the more you laugh the happier, calmer, and healthier you will be.

Laughter reduces the body's level of stress chemicals such as cortisol and adrenaline. When we feel threatened these chemicals help to sharpen our senses: blood vessels constrict and the heart pumps faster so that mind and body can respond to danger—the oft-cited fight-or-flight mechanism. Long-term anxiety and stress result in undesirable levels of these chemicals accumulating in our bodies, leading to stress-related illnesses such as heart attacks.

Laughter reduces blood pressure and increases production of antibodies and the effectiveness of infection-fighting white blood cells. The vibrating of the lungs and diaphragm stimulates muscles, clears the respiratory tract, and provides an internal workout: we breathe more deeply and the inner lining of the blood vessels expands,

increasing blood flow throughout the body, especially to the brain. The result? We're able to think more clearly after a good laugh. Researchers from the University of Maryland have discovered that stress reduces blood flow by 35 percent, while laughter increases it by 22 percent.

ARE CATS SMARTER THAN DOGS?

Cat lovers argue that cats must be smarter than dogs by virtue of their independence and their ability to do largely as they please. Dogs, for example, are often put to work by humans, while cats can sleep all day if they so choose. On the other hand, dogs can be trained to do a host of tasks from sniffing out explosives to locating avalanche victims and pulling a sled. When was the last time you saw eight cats harnessed together, putting in some teamwork?

What does hard science have to say on the matter? Well, researchers have discovered that the structure of the brain is similar in cats and humans. They have the same lobes in the cerebral cortex and identical neurotransmitters, which mean cats process information from their five senses the same way we do. They are adaptable, resourceful, and capable of some very sophisticated learning and decision-making. According to Dr. Julia Albright of Cornell's Veterinary School, "The fact that a cat can adapt to different situations is a sign of intelligence that goes beyond conditioning or instinct."

Cats seem to learn lessons more quickly than dogs. One reprimand or unpleasant outcome is usually enough to discourage a cat from repeating a behavior (or at least teach it to wait until you are out of the room), whereas a dog will often need to have the same instruction drummed into it several times before adapting. Dogs are easier to train than cats, but that is an issue of temperament rather than intelligence.

Not everyone agrees that cats are smarter. Stanley Coren, a psychology professor at the University of British Columbia, says that dogs

are smarter than cats because "If you have two animals that are roughly at the same evolutionary level and roughly the same [classification] . . . the one that has the more complex social structure is almost always brighter."

Perhaps there is no definitive answer to this question since, as with humans, there is a wide spectrum of intelligence among cats and dogs. Some dogs such as Border Collies and German Shepherds are very bright, while Bassett Hounds are notoriously dim-witted. Undoubtedly some dog breeds are smarter than some cat breeds, and vice versa.

WHAT'S LEFT OF A BODY AFTER CREMATION?

When a corpse is cremated it is heated in an industrial furnace powered by fuels such as natural gas and propane to a temperature of between approximately 1,400 and 2,100 degrees Fahrenheit. Since water comprises 70 percent of our bodies, most of the remains vaporize and the gases are discharged through the exhaust system of the furnace. At this point all that's left are ash and dry bone fragments, which are light gray in color and represent about 3.5 percent of the original body mass. In the United States the average weight of the remains is just over 5 pounds for adults.

At a professional crematorium, the bone fragments are swept into a machine called a cremulator which grinds them down to a fine powder. In some countries such as Japan and Taiwan, the bones are left in fragmented form and pulverized only upon request.

The first modern cremation in the United States was very controversial and attracted a lot of attention. It took place on December 6, 1876, in the village of Washington, Pennsylvania, when Baron Joseph Henry Louis Charles De Palm, who had been dead for six months, was cremated under intense media scrutiny with a large crowd of curious locals gathered outside the crematorium. De Palm had been a founder of the Theosophical Society, a group of freethinkers, and he stipulated that his body be cremated in keeping with Eastern tradition. U.S. society was

unaccustomed to this process—press reports variously described the spectacle as "folly," "farce," "objectionable," and "repulsive." We've come a long way since then. Not only do crematoriums present decedents with decorative urns bearing the cremated remains of loved ones, some offer to create synthetic memorial diamonds from carbon separated from the cremated remains of people or pets. The diamonds can be worn as a keepsake by relatives, close friends, or owners.

CAN A DOLPHIN KILL A SHARK?

Dolphins can and do kill small sharks. They will attack large sharks in self-defense, but in a one-on-one match up the odds are greatly stacked in favor of the shark. Given a choice, dolphins will try to avoid sharks rather than attack, and they definitely don't go looking for trouble. Social creatures that they are, however, dolphins will protect their own; they swim in groups (pods), and the largest males will patrol the edge of the pods and chase off sharks.

The idea that dolphins kill sharks persists owing in large part to a very rare incident that took place at the Miami Seaquarium in the 1950s and that was mythologized in the popular television series *Flipper*. Three adult male dolphins attacked a sandbar shark to protect a calf, and ended up killing the predator by butting it repeatedly in its stomach and gills.

During the 1960s, the U.S. Navy trained bottlenose dolphins to injure large sharks by butting their gills, but it seems that the dolphins were highly discerning about which types of sharks they were willing to take on. For example, sandbar, lemon, and nurse sharks were fair game, but the dolphins quickly learned that bull sharks were too dangerous.

Although dolphins and sharks are often seen feeding alongside each other without incident, sharks are known to prey on old or weak dolphins. Hence, another persistent myth about the relationship between dolphins and sharks is that you are less likely to get attacked by a shark if you are swimming with dolphins. If anything, you are in greater danger, since a shark might specifically target you as the

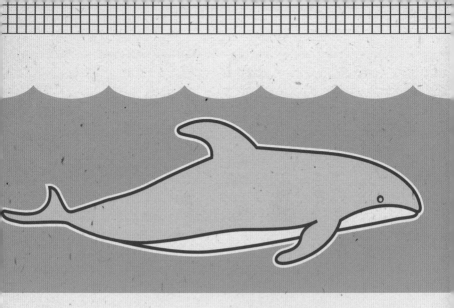

slower, weaker creature.

If you're wondering how a shark would attack, you may be interested to know that a large shark (like a great white) attacking a large dolphin (the killer whale is the biggest) would approach unseen from below and deliver a fatal bite before the dolphin was even aware of its presence.

Bottlenose dolphins are the strongest and most aggressive of the species: a pack could pose a threat to a great white by butting it in its gills, and whipping their tails, but the shark would still be able to severely injure several dolphins. Although the dolphins would have greater maneuverability, the shark would have superior speed and could generally swim away if seriously outnumbered.

DANGER-DOLPHIN

WHAT'S THE MOST DANGEROUS JOB IN THE WORLD?

The chance of an average worker being fatally injured at work is very low. There are approximately 3.9 injuries at work for every 100,000 workers in the United States each year. If you hate your boss, your coworkers get on your nerves, and the office photo-copier is always misbehaving, spare a thought for the following folks who risk their lives every time they punch in.

According to U.S. Bureau of Labor Statistics (BLS), the ten most dan-gerous jobs are as follows (a score of 1 would be equivalent to the average risk of all jobs):

OCCUPATION	RISK FACTOR	GREATEST DANGER
Fishermen	36.3	Drowning
Airplane pilots	22.5	Crashing
Timber cutters	21.05	Being struck by falling objects
Structural iron & steel workers	15.6	Falling
Refuse collectors	10.7	Being crushed
Farmers & ranchers	9.5	Vehicular accidents
Cab drivers	9.5	Homicide
Electrical power-line installers & repairers	8.9	Electrocution
Roofers	8.7	Falling
Construction laborers	8.1	Vehicular accidents & falls

21

You might be surprised to see airline pilots right up there with our blue collar heroes, given the relative infrequency of airplane crashes. Remember, though, that there aren't many pilots in the world, so one fatality relative to overall numbers becomes more significant.

When considering dangerous occupations, we shouldn't overlook stressful jobs, as it is well known that prolonged levels of stress—the "silent killer"—can lead to potentially fatal illnesses. According to the online learning provider Skillsoft, the most stressful jobs in the world are in information technology (IT). One poll of 3,000 IT experts revealed that 97 percent experienced stress on a daily basis, 80 percent reported feeling stressed before they even entered the workplace, and 25 percent had taken time off due to stress.

Here are the top ten most stressful industries, according to SkillSoft:

1. **IT**
2. **Medicine/Healthcare**
3. **Engineering**
4. **Sales and marketing**
5. **Education**
6. **Finance**
7. **Human resources**
8. **Operations**
9. **Production**
10. **Clerical**

This list seems to focus on office jobs (air-traffic controllers, military personnel, and waitresses are conspicuously absent), but office jobs can be extremely stressful. Remember that stress is related to how much control individuals feel that they have over outcomes, rather than how much danger they face.

IS THERE A LIMIT TO THE NUMBER OF TIMES OUR HEARTS CAN BEAT BEFORE WE DIE?

If this were true, which it isn't, it would be a great way to justify not doing any exercise. Why speed up the inevitable end? Then again, even if you believe that exercise extends your life, you may not see the point in spending two years jogging, only to add another two years to your life.

The finite heartbeat theory has often been used to excuse sitting on the couch and watching TV. However, according to the American Heart Association the resting heartbeat of the average person is between 60 and 80 beats per minute (bpm); the fitter you are the lower your resting heartbeat.

Imagine a relatively fit woman who works out five times a week for 30 minutes each time and who has a resting heartbeat of 60 bpm. On days when she doesn't work out her heart will beat 86,400 times.

On days when she exercises, her heart will pump away at 166 bpm for half an hour, so her daily total will be 89,580 beats. During a typical week her heart will beat 620,700 times.

Now take a male couch potato with a resting heartbeat of 75 bpm. Each day his heart beats 108,000 times for a total of 756,000 beats each week, or 135,300 more times than the person who exercises regularly. So even if the finite heartbeat theory were true, it would pay for him to exercise.

1,000 BPM

1,000 BPM

6 BPM

70 BPM

While we definitely don't have a fixed number of heartbeats in us, it is possible to estimate the rough number of heartbeats that occur in an average life. As babies our hearts beat faster and during sleep they slow down, but let's assume an average heart rate of 70 bpm. That gives us an average total of about 100,000 beats each day, about 36 million times each year, and 2.7 billion times over 70 years.

The heart rate of mice and small birds is about 1,000 bpm, and they live about four years. This means their heart beats around 2 billion times, which is quite close to the figure for the average human. However, the heart of a blue whale beats around 6 times a minute, so if the whale's heart were to beat two billion times, it would live for more than 300 years. In short, the finite heartbeat theory is utter bunkum.

DID A MUNCHKIN COMMIT SUICIDE IN THE MOVIE *THE WIZARD OF OZ*?

The story behind this popular legend goes something like this: a hapless actor playing a Munchkin in the 1939 movie *The Wizard of Oz* decided to do himself in during filming after breaking up with his Munchkin girlfriend. Attentive viewers watching a dimly lit stand of trees in the scene in question are apparently treated to the indistinct form of a tiny man setting up a ladder, then kicking it away.

The alleged suicide takes place in the background at the end of the scene where the angry trees shake apples onto Dorothy, the Tin Man, and the Scarecrow. Take a look for yourself and you'll see that the idea isn't totally farfetched: when the three pals link arms and march along the Yellow Brick Road, something definitely happens behind them in the scene, and whatever it is didn't end up on the cutting room floor. So what happened?

The curious occurrence was spotted by moviegoers years ago, and was initially attributed to a clumsy stagehand falling out of a tree. However, when the fiftieth-anniversary video of the movie was released in 1989, increasing numbers of viewers were able to freeze-frame the event and the Munchkincide theory exploded.

The reality is more straightforward, though no less interesting. During filming, several birds of various sizes were borrowed from the Los

Angeles Zoo and allowed to roam around the set to give it an outdoor feel. Perhaps you've noticed the peacock strutting around the Tin Man's shack while he is being oiled back to life. While Dorothy and her friends skipped off to the Emerald City, one of these big birds in the background (probably a crane) pecked the floor and then flapped its wings, assuring itself a small place in cinematic history. If you still aren't convinced, it might be worth mentioning that this scene was filmed weeks before the Munchkins had even arrived for theirs.

Die-hard conspiracy theorists argue that the real suicide takes place in Munchkinland. We'll leave this for you to investigate.

WHAT WOULD THE WORLD BE LIKE IF ALL HUMANS SUDDENLY DISAPPEARED?

The idea of a world without humans is not so farfetched. Ninety-nine percent of all species that have ever lived are now extinct, and human beings have existed for only a mere fraction of the Earth's 4.5-billion-year history.

If we were all to disappear tomorrow, the infrastructure of our civilization would disintegrate with alarming speed. Within hours of our departure lights would go out around the globe as power-generating plants, deprived of workers to supply them with fossil fuels, would start shutting down. Nuclear power stations would power down automatically with no one using their electricity. The only large-scale power plant that would continue to run for more than a few months is the Hoover Dam, which would operate automatically for a few years until a build-up of mussels blocked the cooling tunnels, causing the turbines to overheat and shut down.

Without electricity and maintenance, underground tunnels in cities would flood within 36 hours, as water pumps failed. (In New York's subway system alone, 700 pumps currently remove 13 million gallons of water each day.)

Within six months urban areas would turn wild as predators—including coyotes, bobcats, and larger carnivores such as bears—returned to colonize them. Within a year vegetation would have already begun to reclaim towns and cities, and sunk its roots into tarmac and buildings, breaking up their foundations and structure. Wildfires would rage unchecked and entire neighborhoods would burn down.

Within five years New York's Central Park—which covers 843 acres—would resemble a small jungle of saplings as it returned to its earlier swampy conditions; within twenty years concrete buildings would begin to crumble and many cities, especially low-lying ones like London and Amsterdam, would be flooded. Within forty years most timber-framed buildings (i.e., 90 percent of the homes in the U.S.) would have either burned or rotted.

Within a century, without maintenance, large engineered structures such as the Brooklyn Bridge would rust away and collapse. Meanwhile, a vertical ecosystem of wildlife (birds, snakes, cats) would inhabit the vine-covered skyscrapers. Metal-framed buildings would collapse after 300 years; the largest concrete structures would disintegrate within 500 years. After a millennium there would be little evidence left of where our cities once stood.

Without proper storage conditions our digital recorded media, such as DVDs and film (acetate), would last for fewer than 100 years; books might last several hundred. Even terrestrial radio broadcasts that travel out into space would dissipate into unintelligible noise before reaching the nearest star.

After humankind was gone for 10,000 years—a mere blip of time on the geological chronometer—there would be very little evidence that our species ever existed. Large stone structures such as the Great Wall of China, the Pyramid at Giza (by now buried by sand), and possibly the Hoover Dam would be among a handful of remnants of our civilization.

WHY CAN'T I TICKLE MYSELF?

Most people are ticklish, but very few are able to tickle themselves. (Most likely something isn't working properly in the brains of those who can.) Being ticklish is a natural defense: it's what makes us brush away creepy crawlies or respond to physical contact from an external source that might be a threat. However, the brain anticipates a self-tickle because it knows that (for example) your right hand is about to dig you in the ribs; consequently, you won't respond with the customary agitation that comes when someone else tickles you. The brain needs to be able to distinguish between sensations that are self-generated and those stimulated by external sources so that it can filter out unnecessary stimuli. The brain continually receives an enormous amount of sensory information, and if it paid everything equal attention it would be overwhelmed and its functioning compromised.

For example, when you are typing on a keyboard, you need to be able to concentrate on what you are thinking rather than the feel of the keys on your fingertips; whereas it's important that you respond to someone tapping you on the back, as this could signal a threat. Brain scientists have located the part of the brain responsible for making these distinctions: it's the cerebellum, located at the back of the part of the brain that monitors our movements.

An inability to distinguish between self-generated and external stimuli is a characteristic of schizophrenia. Many people with schizophrenia think they are being touched, even when they aren't, and they have auditory hallucinations, both of which indicate an impaired ability to self-monitor. Most of us can distinguish easily between a thought in our own heads and the sound of someone else talking. In tests, schizophrenic subjects experience the same degree of ticklishness from tickles that are self-administered as those that are externally generated.

DO COWS PRODUCE MORE MILK WHEN THEY LISTEN TO CLASSICAL MUSIC THAN WHEN THEY LISTEN TO ROCK 'N' ROLL?

Yes. They also prefer country to rock. It seems that cows would rather listen to mood music than to something with a strong fast beat. And in case you think that is udderly unfounded, you'll be relieved to discover that the question was answered by a ten-year-old boy, who won first place in a regional science fair for his efforts.

Daniel McElmurray lives on a dairy farm in Augusta, Georgia. In 2003, after hearing his father complain about the amount of milk his cows were producing, Daniel decided to test the effect of three different types of music on milk yield: classical, rock, and country. The cows were accustomed to being milked to the sound of music, as Daniel and his father always had some-thing playing while they worked. For his experiment he played Lynyrd Skynyrd, Shania Twain, and various classical pieces. The cows responded to the classical music by producing 1,000 pounds more of milk. Rock music proved the least productive. Daniel's explanation: "I guess a slower beat helps them relax."

Contemporaneous research in the United Kingdom corroborated these findings. Psychologists at Leicester University played music of different tempos to herds of Friesian cows. Beethoven's *Pastoral Symphony* and "Moon River" had a very positive effect on milk yield, while up-tempo tracks such as Bananarama's "Venus" and Wonderstuff's "Size of a Cow" actually reduced yield when compared to that of cows that listened to no music at all. The study's leader, Dr. Adrian North, explained the results: "Calming music can improve yield, probably because it reduces stress." During the 9-week experiment the researchers measured an increase of 3 percent in milk yield in cows that listened to music with a slow tempo for 12 hours a day every day.

WHY DO SALMON SWIM UPSTREAM TO SPAWN?

The urge to reproduce is in the DNA of every animal, including salmon. The only difference between salmon and other animals is that they have to return upstream to the spawning grounds before mating, ensuring that only the strongest specimens survive to reproduce. They are guided by a chemical memory to follow a trail of minute traces of pheromones home to their birthplace. Most salmon, male and female, die shortly after mating, so most baby salmon are born as orphans.

Why go to all that effort to reach the spawning grounds? Why not breed in places that are easier to reach? While they are swimming upstream, adult salmon don't eat. Instead they manage to live on their fat reserves even while they expend a considerable amount of energy fighting the current and negotiating obstacles such as waterfalls, rocks, anglers, and bears. Why bother?

Because the shallow, calm waters of the spawning grounds make them the best places to mate and deposit and incubate eggs. The water further downstream is deeper, its currents are stronger, and its temperature is more variable. However, the shallow waters upstream make the fish more vulnerable to attack from predators.

While the male salmon swims around aggressively protecting his patch, the female swishes her tail back and forth to create a gravel nest on the stream bed (called a "redd") where she lays her eggs. After the male fertilizes

the eggs the female covers them with gravel. When the eggs hatch the baby fish begin to make their way downstream and by the time they reach the open sea they are developed enough to face the hazards that await them there. Some salmon stay out at sea for up to five years before returning to the fresh water to spawn and die.

WHY DO SOME PREGNANT WOMEN EAT COAL?

Unusual cravings are common during pregnancy and their incidence appears to be on the rise. In a recent survey of pregnant women, three-quarters admitted to experiencing a craving, compared to a little less than one-third 50 years ago.

Coal is quite high up the list of unusual cravings. The same poll placed ice at the top, craved by 22 percent of the women, followed closely by coal at 17 percent. Other cravings included toothpaste (9 percent), mud (7 percent), chalk (6 percent), and laundry soap (5 percent). One percent of women reported a craving for rubber.

The condition of experiencing non-food cravings is called "pica," named for the Latin for magpie, the waste disposal unit of the bird world that is renowned for eating just about anything. Pica often occurs in childhood, and it is displayed more frequently in pregnant women who have a history of pica in their family or childhood.

It has been suggested that these cravings are a sign of deficiency in vital vitamins and minerals, but often the items that are craved do not provide any supplements, and can actually be harmful. The reason for bizarre cravings is still not completely understood, but it is likely to be connected to altered hormone levels and the dulled sense of taste that pregnant women often experience.

In Kenya pregnant women commonly crave soft stones called "odowa" which are sold in the markets specifically to satisfy these unusual urges. The stones are reported to have a floury taste, but their abrasive texture may also be part of the attraction. However, if the stones are chewed and swallowed without adequate water they can cause kidney and liver problems. Although experts attribute the popularity of eating odowa to deficiencies of minerals such as calcium, the stones are quite low in this mineral; they do, however, provide magnesium.

WAS THE CURSE
OF TUTANKHAMUN
FOR REAL?

On April 5, 1923, Lord Carnarvon, the wealthy benefactor who funded Howard Carter's forays around the Valley of the Kings in Luxor, Egypt, died from pneumonia after nicking a mosquito bite while shaving. Just seven weeks earlier he had presided over the breaking of the seals on the burial chamber of Tutankhamun. Two days after he died the mummy was inspected and a small mark was discovered on its face in exactly the same place as the mosquito bite. It is said that as Carnarvon died the lights went out in Cairo (a not unusual occurrence) and his pet dog in London howled and died at the same time. It appeared that Marie Corelli, the novelist who had warned that bad things would happen to anyone who entered the tomb, had been proved correct, and rumors began to circulate that the "Pharaoh's Curse" had claimed its first victims.

Another part of the story claims that on the day that Howard Carter opened the tomb, his pet canary was eaten by a cobra (one of the protectors of the tomb). In fact the canary lived for many years. Arthur Mace, one of the archaeologists on the same trip, died from suspected arsenic poisoning in 1923.

The wealthy financier and railroad executive George Gould died of pneumonia on May 16, 1923, on the French Riviera, after visiting the tomb. The following year, radiologist Archibald Reid, who X-rayed the mummy to determine its age, returned to England complaining of fatigue, and died soon after. Carnarvon's secretary, Richard Bethell, died of heart failure four months after the tomb was opened; five months after Carnarvon's death his half-brother Aubrey Herbert died of peritonitis. In 1966 Mohammed Ibrahim, Egypt's director of antiquities, who is alleged to have suffered nightmares about what would happen if the artifacts left the country, was run over by a car and died. In 1972 the then director of antiquities, Dr. Gamal Mehrez, died the night after he supervised packing of the items for transport by the Royal Air Force; several crew members were supposedly injured as well.

Hearing the list of deaths related to the exploration of Pharaoh's tomb could certainly lead one to suspect some kind of curse. The truth is that Carnarvon, the man whose death started all this nonsense, was an old man in failing health with an already compromised immune system. The newspapers pounced on the curse idea and one claimed that the words "They who enter this sacred tomb shall swift be visited by wings of death" were

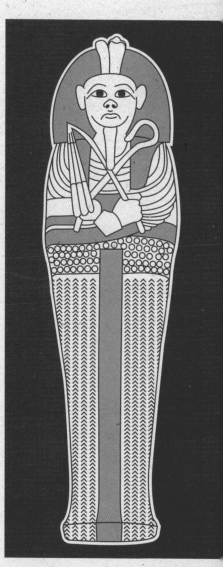

inscribed at the entrance to the tomb. No such inscription existed. On one of the tomb's artifacts, a custodian jackal, was written, "It is I who hinder the sand from choking the secret chamber. I am for the protection of the deceased," to which an imaginative reporter added, ". . . and I will kill all those who cross this threshold into the sacred precincts of the Royal King who lives forever."

Of the twenty-six people who were present at the opening of the tomb, only six died within the next decade. Many lived to an old age. Howard Carter survived until March 1939, seventeen years after entering the tomb. Carnarvon's daughter, Lady Evelyn Herbert, entered the tomb with him shortly after its discovery but did not die until 1980 when she was in her late seventies.

A mummy's curse was already a well-known literary motif dating back decades before Lord Carnarvon's death. The first story featuring a malevolent mummy was written by Jane Loudon Webb in 1821. Towards the end of the nineteenth century many novelists, including Louisa May Alcott (author of *Little Women*) wrote about cursed mummies. Both Arthur Conan Doyle, author of the Sherlock Holmes stories, and the less-well-known writer Marie Corelli, suggested in interviews and letters that Tutankhamun's tomb might be cursed.

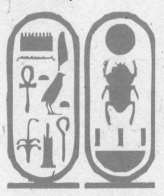

IS TIME TRAVEL THEORETICALLY POSSIBLE?

Before the Large Hadron Collider (LHC) in Cern, Switzerland, was fired up on September 10, 2008, two Russian mathematicians predicted that it might create tiny wormholes in space-time—the conditions necessary for time travel. If their predictions come true, it may be the first step towards building a time machine that would allow people from the future to come back to our present to visit us. At the time an article in *New Scientist* conceded, "The slim possibility remains that we will see visitors from the future in the next year."

Few people really believe that the LHC will make time travel possible. Even if wormholes are created they will be subatomic (hence too small for anyone to pass through) and last only for a fraction of a second. Still, some believe that might be all the opportunity an advanced civilization needs to pay us a visit.

Physicists only began seriously working on the idea of creating wormholes in the space-time continuum in 1986, when the American astronomer Carl Sagan, gathering research for his novel *Contact*, asked his cosmologist friend Kip Thorne to devise a way for his characters to cover long distances without traveling faster than the speed of light. Thorne came up with the idea of manipulating black holes to create wormholes, opening up an exciting new avenue of research.

The laws of physics and Albert Einstein's General Theory of Relativity do not prohibit time travel, but the practicalities are another matter. Newton thought that time traveled in a straight line, but Einstein demonstrated that time meanders like a river and that time-space can be curved by massive objects with huge gravitational fields, such as stars. Einstein doubted the possibility of time travel, but his colleague Kurt Gödel used his equations to show that time travel is at least theoretically possible.

According to the Theory of Relativity, time slows down as you approach a black hole because its huge gravitational field bends space-time, like an apple sitting on a piece of saran wrap. Also, the closer you get to the speed of light, the more time slows, until, at the speed of light, time stops. Einstein showed that time isn't a fixed linear constant—it is relative to the observer.

The biggest theoretical obstacles to time travel are the paradoxes it creates. The obvious one is going back in time and changing history so that either you or the version of the future you came from cease to exist. Scientists have solved this paradox with the "multiverse" model, which suggests that there are an infinite number of universes to cater to the infinite number of possible outcomes.

Another argument against time travel is that there is no record of it happening. Some people argue that it has taken place without our knowledge, however, speculating that extraterrestrials are time travelers or that visitors from another time kept a low profile.

Amazingly, subatomic particles do already travel back in time. When an electron absorbs a photon, it sends out another photon. This process is responsible for the scattering of light. However, it is also possible for an electron to emit a photon before it has absorbed one, and even travel back in time to absorb a photon. These backward-moving electrons are anti-particles called positrons, because unlike regular electrons, they have a positive charge. Weird and seemingly impossible things happen at a subatomic quantum level, for sure, but that doesn't mean we can apply these principles to the larger world.

ARE MULTI-BLADE RAZORS BETTER THAN SINGLE-BLADE RAZORS?

Do you sometimes suspect that the disposable razor market has gone crazy? We're now up to cartridges with five blades (and counting), and the prices have risen accordingly. Let's get back to basics and find out whether two, three, four, or—heaven help us—five blades are better than just one.

The principle behind twin-blade razors is that the first blade cuts through the whisker and pulls the hair out from the follicle slightly; before it can retract, the second blade cuts it even more closely. However, no razor company has ever provided clinical proof for this claim. Also, as we all know, the cut stubble gets stuck in between the blades, which means you have to rinse often, and throw away the razor long before the blade becomes blunt.

Fewer strokes are supposed to create less irritation, but there is little difference between the number of strokes made with a two-blade or a five-blade razor. If a shave takes sixty strokes of a single blade, then it should only take twelve strokes with a five-blader—which is patently absurd. The pricing model is the same that the manufacturers of printers use: sell the unit cheap, then charge a premium for expensive consumables. The handle and the first few blades may seem like a bargain, but thereafter the price paid versus incremental improvement in shaving invokes the law of diminishing of returns.

Over the last thirty years razor manufacturers have also reduced the quality of their blades. A Consumer's Research report in 1978 claimed that a disposable razor could be used ten times; by 1981 this number had slumped to four.

Bearing all this in mind, do you really think that the multinational companies that offer you four and five blades really care about you and your skin? Our advice is to stick with a twin-blader with a swiveling head.

WHO INVENTED ZERO?

If you want to split hairs and call this a trick question, then the answer is no one "invented" zero, since it was sort of always there and just needed discovering. Then again, numbers are a human construct, so there is a strong argument that someone indeed invented it, since the number zero is very different from the concept of nothing.

The idea of nothing, or "not having," must have been in people's minds as soon as numbers were invented. What was lacking for so many years was a special symbol for zero to bring it into the number line.

We know that the Babylonians used a space (and later a symbol of two slanted wedges) as a placeholder for empty "columns" as far back as 1700 B.C. They wrote in cuneiform, a system which relied on making a series of marks on soft clay tablets, leaving a space in the clay to indicate a place without value. They didn't, however, view the space as a number itself. It was seen rather as *the lack of a number*, which is not the same

thing as the modern number zero. The Babylonians didn't use their zero symbol on its own or at the end of a number.

Independent of the Babylonians, the Mayans had developed the concept of zero by 36 B.C. and used a shell-shaped figure to signify it. There is some evidence to suggest that a neighboring Mesoamerican civilization such as the Olmec may have used a zero symbol even earlier.

In the second century A.D., the ancient Greeks devised a symbol for zero—a small circle with a long overbar—which they used alone rather than as a placeholder. They were very uncomfortable with the paradox of something being nothing, however, and restricted the zero to the fractional part of a number, rather than including it among the integrals.

The truly modern concept of zero as a number rather than a symbol for separation didn't really blossom until the ninth century in India. The Indians embraced both the philosophical and spiritual significance of zero, as well as its concrete existence. They performed practical calculations with it, and treated it as a separate number in its own right, with none of the philosophical reservations that plagued the Greeks.

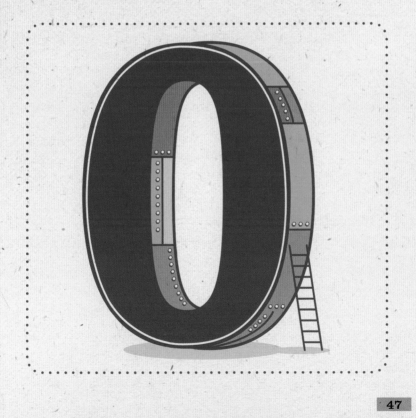

WHY DO GOLF BALLS HAVE DIMPLES?

The aerodynamic forces at work as a golf ball travels through the air have a major impact on the distance that it travels. Early golf balls, called featheries, were simple leather pouches stuffed with goose feathers. The stitches were on the inside which left the outside very smooth; it was believed that this would create less drag. The ball was oiled and painted white. The next innovation was the gutta-percha ball, made from the gum of the Malaysian Sapodilla tree that was heated and shaped into a smooth sphere.

Golfers started to notice that battered old balls with nicks and dents traveled further than new smooth ones and manufacturers began designing golf balls with grooves, dimples, and scratches. By the late 1920s, a pattern of dimples was widely accepted as the standard design. Most modern golf balls have between 300 and 500 dimples arranged uniformly and symmetrically.

The dimples act as "turbulators" that introduce turbulence in the surrounding layer of air as the ball passes through it. Usually turbulence is a bad thing, but in the case of a traveling sphere it is beneficial.

The place where the air slides around a traveling object is called the "boundary layer." If the object has a very aerodynamic shape, such as a bullet, the air follows its contours, and the drag is kept to a minimum. However, in the case of a sphere, which is less aerodynamic, the air separates from the ball, causing turbulence behind it and slowing it down. If the ball is smooth the laminar flow of air separates early. When the ball has dimples the resulting turbulence means that the separation occurs slightly later, making the separation region behind the ball much smaller. This causes less drag, which translates as greater speed.

DOES THE WORD "SUPERCALIFRAGILIS-TICEXPIALIDOCIOUS" PREDATE THE MOVIE *MARY POPPINS*?

Yes. In 1965 Wonderland Music, who published the song from the Walt Disney movie, were sued for copyright infringement by songwriters Gloria Parker and Barney Young, writers of the 1951 "Super Song," which uses the word "Supercalafajalistick-espeealadojus" and was recorded by Alan Holmes and the New Tones on Columbia Records. They also claimed to have shown their song to Disney in 1951. Wonderland Music won its case partly on the basis that "variants of the word were known . . . many years prior to 1949."

The word "supercalifragilis" crops up in the 1942 movie *The Undying Monster*. The character Rob Curtis describes a female character as having "an overactive supercalifragilis," which he defines as "female intuition."

Supercalifragilisticexpialidocious does not appear in any form in any of the original books written by P.L. Travers between 1934 and 1952 (*Mary Poppins*, *Mary Poppins Comes Back*, *Mary Poppins Opens the Door*, and *Mary Poppins in the Park*). Incidentally the movie, largely based on the first book, was such a disappointment to Travers that she forbade any sequels (she disliked the music, hated the use of animation, and felt that Mary Poppins' character had been over-simplified).

Brothers Robert and Richard Sherman wrote the song for *Mary Poppins*, and in an interview with the website Laist™ on November 2, 2007, Richard claimed that they invented the word together: "That's a word we sort of concocted from our childhood when we used to make up double talk words." However, in their book *Walt's Time: From Be-fore to Beyond,* published in 1988, the brothers say they were intro-duced to the word "super-cadja-flawjalistic-espealedojus" at a summer camp in the Adirondack Mountains when they were boys in the mid-1930s. They believed the word "had been passed down in many variations through many generations of kids."

HAS ANYONE EVER DIED FROM PICKING HIS OR HER NOSE?

There is a familiar story about a man who was picking his nose while driving. Someone shunted into him from behind and his finger went through his nose and into his brain, killing him instantly. However, you won't find it in any newspaper archive or medical journal; it's probably an urban legend. Thousands of people do pick their nose while they are driving, and according to a recent survey by Response Insurance, 17 percent of Americans admitted that they have nearly caused an accident by picking their nose behind the wheel. With a figure of near misses that high, it is very likely that a sizeable number of crashes have been caused by nose picking, whether drivers admit it or not, and some of these may have caused fatalities.

Is it possible to sustain a fatal injury simply by picking your nose, sitting in the relative safety of an armchair watching TV? In fact it is possible, but you'd have to have a sturdy and forceful rummage with a pointed implement such as a pair of scissors. Deep inside the nose, at the roof between the two orbits (eye sockets), sits the ethmoid bone, which separates the nasal cavity from the brain. It is thin and delicate and it can easily be injured by a sharp blow to the nose, which can drive pieces of bone into the brain tissue. Normal nose picking would not rupture the ethmoid bone, but using tools other than your finger greatly increases the risk, especially if someone hits your arm sharply.

Excessive nose picking leads to soreness, inflammation of the nasal tissue, and bleeding. If picking breaks the skin, there is a slim chance that bacteria could enter the body, block blood flow in the nose, and lead to a large blood clot within the cavernous sinus. This would have been fatal before the introduction of antibiotics and modern surgical drainage techniques. In very rare cases nose picking could also cause a fatal nosebleed.

WHY DON'T WOMEN GO BALD?

Women do lose their hair, but in a different way than do men. Women's hair thins all over the scalp, whereas men experience "male pattern baldness": the hair recedes from the forehead above the temples and thins on the crown of the head, eventually progressing to partial or complete baldness.

There has been a great deal of research into baldness in men. A variety of genetic and environmental factors contribute to it, but hormones are one of the key components, especially androgens such as dihydrotestosterone (DHT) which play an important role in male development in utero and during puberty. Androgens regulate hair growth and men have much higher levels of these hormones than do women.

Hair growth is a complicated biological process that involves more than a hundred genes and scientists still have plenty to learn about it. We know that hair grows about

a half-inch per month and that each hair grows for between two to six years until it stops growing and falls out. At that point the hair follicle starts producing a new hair. Androgens interfere with this process, and cause the hair follicles to shrink and/or die, reducing their ability to grow healthy strands.

If you are a man losing your hair you have your mother to thank, since the susceptibility to baldness is passed down through the maternal line. If you are bald, it's a safe bet that your maternal grandfather was also follically-challenged. Men with male pattern baldness generally have lower overall levels of

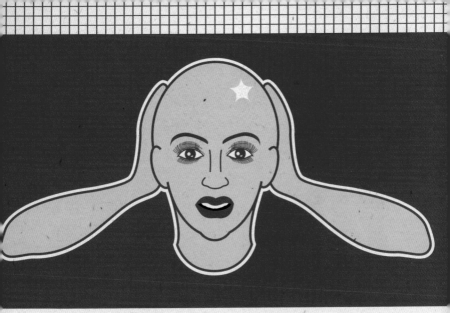

testosterone than other men, but higher levels of "unbound testosterone" and DHT.

Lifestyle also contributes to hair loss. After the Second World War, baldness dramatically increased in the Japanese population as diets became higher in fat and calories and exercise decreased. Regular vigorous aerobic exercise (jogging or swimming, for example, rather than bodybuilding) helps to reduce baldness by lowering levels of unbound testosterone and DHT.

Hair loss in women is on the increase in western society. While male pattern baldness usually begins in early middle age, in women baldness can happen at any time if their hormones are out of whack or if their bodies are under great stress. Women with polycystic ovary syndrome, for example, suffer hair loss, but it can also occur after childbirth, a crash diet, or a traumatic event.

HOW BIG IS
WHALE POOP?

Whales poop a lot. Although some scientists study them as their life's work, whale feces are difficult to measure because whales excrete mostly diarrhea—tonnes (metric tons) of it.

Whale dung, which is usually brown, orange, or neon-red, contains some chunks, but the largest of these weigh about a pound. Whales poop about 3 percent of their body mass every day, so for a 180-tonne whale that's about the weight of two Humvees! They swallow a lot of sea water, so what comes out the other end is runny. Perhaps that is a blessing; passing a military troop carrier morning and evening would be an eye-watering challenge even for a blue whale.

Measuring whale scat is one of the most important and challenging jobs in the field of conservation. You can learn a lot from whales by looking at their feces: what they like to eat, where they eat, health and stress levels, genetics, hormones, whether they have parasites, and even whether a female is pregnant.

Rather than sail around aimlessly looking for large reddish brown stains in the ocean, scientists use sniffer dogs trained to track down fresh poop from up to a mile away. They rush to collect samples before it dissolves and disperses, as whale poop floats around for about an hour after it's released.

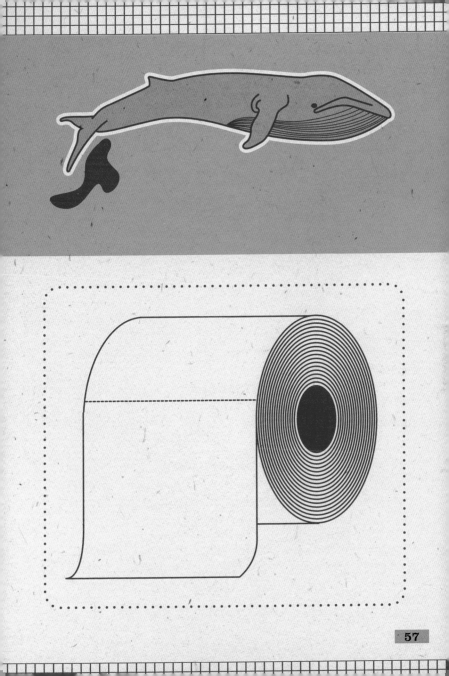

WHAT'S THE ORIGIN OF GIVING SOMEONE THE FINGER?

When Kate Winslet flipped Leonardo DiCaprio the bird in the movie *Titanic*, many viewers thought it was anachronistic. In fact, the one-finger salute is much older than you might think. The earliest recorded reference to the use of the extended middle finger in an obscene gesture appears in *The Clouds*, a comic play by the Greek writer Aristophanes written in 423 B.C. However, it is likely that its origins go back even further than this.

An urban myth places the origin of giving the middle finger at the Battle of Agincourt in 1415, when the French made it known that they would cut off the middle fingers of the English archers, so that they could no longer draw the longbow. After their victory, the English mocked the vanquished French by displaying that their middle fingers were still very much intact.

There are many references in Roman literature to the *digitus infamis* or *digitus impudicus* (infamous or obscene finger). For example,

one of Martial's epigrams advises, "Laugh loudly, Sextillus, when someone calls you a queen and put your middle finger out." The mad emperor Caligula is reported to have enjoyed humiliating his subjects by proffering his middle finger instead of his hand for them to kiss. Among Mediterranean cultures, during the first century A.D. the *digitus impudicus* was also used to ward off the evil eye.

Flipping the bird fell out of fashion for hundreds of years, but appears to have experienced a renaissance in U.S. popular culture towards the end of the nineteenth century. The earliest photo of someone giving the finger is a team picture of the Boston Beaneaters snapped in 1886, in which Charles "Old Hoss" Radbourn, standing at the top left of the frame, brazenly stuck one up just behind the shoulders of his seated teammates.

HOW CAN YOU GET CRYONICALLY FROZEN?

The American Cryonics Society offers a service to freeze human bodies and store them until medical science has advanced sufficiently to resuscitate them. You can even buy insurance plans that pay for this procedure upon your death.

Getting frozen cryonically is the easy (albeit expensive) part; it's not sustaining cell damage while being frozen, and then getting thawed out and reanimated, that eludes scientists, who are still years away from making it a reality. At present, they are struggling with the less ambitious goal of damage-free cryopreservation of organs such as the liver and heart.

Cryopreservation is a process that involves preserving cells and tissues by cooling them to subzero temperatures (typically minus 320 degrees Fahrenheit, the boiling point of liquid nitrogen). This ar-rests all biological activity (and therefore biodegradation). Howev-er, when tissues are cooled slowly, they lose water and ice forms be-tween the cells, which distorts and damages them, much the same as ice bursting a water pipe. Cryo-protectants can be added to lower the freezing temperature; instead of crystallizing you will then get a thick solution that turns into amor-phous ice, which causes less dam-age. However, the cryoprotectants are themselves destructive. All in all things don't look promising for the handful of gullible folk who have already paid to have their bodies frozen.

So far no large animal has been cryopreserved for any significant amount of time and successfully brought back to life. Veterinary surgeon Mike Duggan has drained the blood of pigs, replaced it with chilled organ-preservation fluid, and then revived the animals hours later, but this process merely slows the metabolism. It wouldn't stop putrefaction if the animals were to be kept in this state for several months or years.

WHY DOES RIGOR MORTIS HAPPEN AND HOW LONG DOES IT LAST?

Rigor mortis is the stiffening of the body that takes place shortly after death. It is caused by contraction of the skeletal muscles, which are unable to relax, locking the joints in place. It starts with the facial muscles and spreads to the rest of the body, beginning between two to three hours after death.

At a microscopic level, muscles are made up of thick filaments of protein called myosin, and thick filaments of a protein called actin. Whenever you decide to move your body, your brain sends a nerve impulse to the relevant muscles, setting off a biochemical reaction that makes the myosin filaments stick to the actin filaments. When thousands of filaments stick together at the same time, the muscle contracts, moving the bones and joints that it surrounds. The filaments stay stuck until another molecule, ad-

enosine triphosphate (ATP), is introduced. The ATP attaches itself to the myosin and makes it let go of the actin. As long as a person is alive and breathing, his or her body continually produces ATP.

When a person dies, the walls of the muscle cells become more permeable to calcium ions, which are the bridge that makes the filaments stick together. Calcium ions flow into the muscle cells and trigger the filament sticking, but there is no ATP present to relax them (by flushing out the calcium

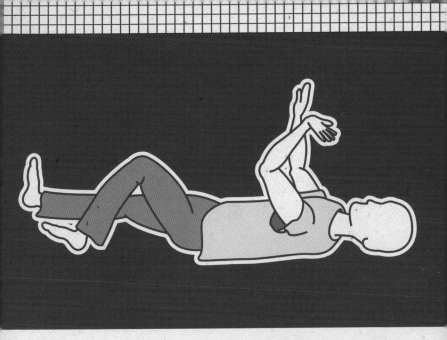

ions) because ATP is produced by respiration, which has ceased. So the muscles get tighter and tighter. Maximum stiffness occurs between twelve to twenty-four hours after death. The muscles stay locked up until decomposition occurs. Decomposition begins immediately after death, so rigor mortis only lasts about seventy-two hours, after which the muscle filaments have decomposed sufficiently that they no longer can stick together.

HOW DO INTERNET COOKIES WORK?

Cookies are simple text files that are stored on your hard drive when you visit websites (as long as your browser is set to enable cookies). Internet cookies are not programs or applications and they are intrinsically neither good nor bad. Most cookies just store basic information such as a unique user ID so that the host can track how many hits a website is getting. Others store more information, such as the contents of a shopping basket for an online retailer. Cookies can't access other parts of your computer, search your hard drive, or perform any other intrusive functions.

When you visit a website, your browser checks for a cookie in your cookies folder on your hard drive. If it finds one it sends the cookie data to the website; otherwise it sends nothing. The website responds by accessing the cookie data, which it then updates during your visit. If this is your first visit or if you have recently deleted the cookies from your cookie folder, it creates a cookie containing a new user ID.

Companies also use cookies to record which advertising banners have appeared while you browse, allowing them to go through a cycle of ads, rather than repeat the same ones. If you accept a webpage's offer to remember personal details, such as your username or address, these will be stored on a cookie.

Cookies can also be used to store your preferences, allowing you to customize your browsing experience by changing the content and/or layout. The problem with cookies is that some are visible on multiple sites, and companies can share these, allowing them to cross reference information about you and build up a huge profile. Privacy issues have always been associated with cookies, but most modern browsers have the option to block or filter them.

HOW CAN THE GIDEONS AFFORD TO PUT A BIBLE IN EVERY HOTEL ROOM?

Look in the nightstand drawer in just about any hotel worldwide and you'll probably find a Bible that has been left by the Gideons International. They've been providing Bibles free of charge to hotels, motels, military bases, prisons, schools, and hospitals for a century—an estimated 56 million of them every year. So how can they afford it and how do they convince so many establishments to accept them?

In September of 1889 traveling salesmen John H. Nicholson and Samuel E. Hill were obliged to share a room in the crowded Boscobel hotel in Boscobel, Wisconsin. After discovering they were both Christians they read the Bible together and discussed forming a Christian traveling men's association. In July they were joined by a third salesman, William J. Knights, and founded the Gideons. The primary focus of the Gideons was personal evangelization and introducing others to the Lord Jesus Christ. It wasn't until eleven years later that the Gideons got the idea to place Bibles in hotel rooms, and a further eight years that this was put into practice. After that they lost no time; during the next two decades the organization distributed one million Bibles. Today the Gideons International has more than 140,000 members worldwide, and it receives millions of dollars each year from Evangelical churches around the globe. In total, the organization has given away an estimated 1.4 billion Bibles translated into 83 languages.

In a predominantly Christian country such as the United States it isn't too difficult to see why hotels accept the Bibles. Whenever a new hotel opens the Gideons formally present the proprietor with a copy of the Bible and enough copies for each room; the latter are distributed by the housekeeping staff. Despite the fact that large numbers of American adults have disaffiliated themselves from organized religions, Christians still account for more than 80 percent of the population, which any new business offends at its peril.

Increasingly, in the interest of religious and cultural diversity, hotels are offering additional religious works such as the Quran and the Torah. But the Gideon Bible is here to stay. According to Joe McInerney, chief executive of American Hotel & Lodging Association, "It's been in the U.S. lodging industry for so long—when you open a hotel it's one of those things on your checklist . . . it's right up there with soap."

HOW LIKELY IS IT THAT AN ASTEROID WILL DESTROY LIFE ON EARTH?

Hundreds of thousands of meteors enter the Earth's atmosphere every day, but most burn up before they can reach the ground. Impact with a really big asteroid occurs much more rarely. Every hundred thousand years or so a Near-Earth Object (NEO) larger than one half mile wide hits the Earth, and every hundred million years the Earth gets hit by an NEO larger than 3 miles wide. The last time a really big asteroid hit the Earth was about 67 million years ago and it may have been responsible for the extinction of the dinosaurs. We should be expecting the next one some time during the next 30 million years.

Fifty thousand years ago a meteor hit Earth near what is now Flagstaff, Arizona, leaving an impact crater three-quarters of a mile wide and 700 feet deep. The resulting explosion was comparable to that of an atom bomb; life on Earth carried on regardless. However, if Earth was hit by an asteroid 3 miles wide, weighing trillions of tons, and traveling at a speed of 50,000 miles an hour, most of the life on the planet would be extinguished. The shockwaves would level cities, generate hurricanes, and create tidal waves hundreds of feet high. The air temperature would rise to over 500 degrees Fahrenheit, the surface of the oceans would boil, and then the temperature would plummet to below freezing after dust thrown into the atmosphere blocked the sun's rays. It would take several months for the dust

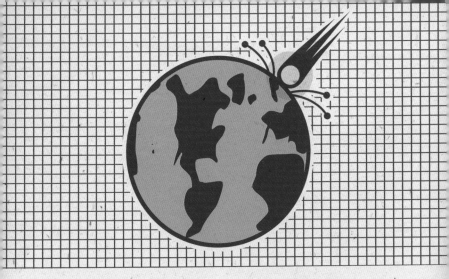

to begin to settle, allowing some light in, but by then all plant life and most animals would be dead.

NASA estimates that there are about 2,000 NEOs in space that are larger than half a mile in diameter. So far only about 10 percent have been identified. NASA has been keeping a particularly close watch on Apophis, an asteroid 1,300 feet wide, since its discovery in 2004. It will pass close to Earth in 2012, and when it passes us again on April 13, 2029 (a Friday, naturally), the Earth's gravity will deflect its orbit. There is a 1-in-5,500 chance that this could set the asteroid on a collision course the next time it appears in 2036. Scientists are warning that we need to start planning how to deflect it now. The use of explosives has been ruled out because this would scatter debris over a wide area. Possible alternatives include crashing a spacecraft into the asteroid at a high speed, or changing the asteroid's color, which would reflect more of the sun's rays, changing its course gradually over several years.

Asteroids may have played a significant role in the creation of the universe by bringing the first carbon-based molecules to Earth. If there really is a giant rock hurtling through outer space with our name on it, it would be a cruel irony indeed if that asteroid were to end life too.

DO MY EARS EVER STOP GROWING?

Have you ever wondered why old people have such big ears that stick out? Is it because their heads shrink when they get old, or that they have less hair, making their ears appear bigger? Or could it be something altogether more alarming—is it possible that our ears never stop growing?

To answer the question, you must first understand what an ear is made of. The outer ear is mostly made of cartilage and skin, with a little fat and muscle. Does the cartilage and skin continue to grow throughout life? Yes, and no. The cells divide, grow, mature, and die, just like cells elsewhere in our bodies, but the cartilage doesn't grow in size.

So what's going on here? Could it be that the earlobes thicken and droop downwards (since body fat usually increase with age, and skin sags), creating the illusion of growth?

In July 1993, nineteen British doctors tried to settle the matter once and for all. They studied 206 patients ranging from ages thirty to ninety-three, with a mean age of 53.75 years and a median age of fifty-three. In each case they measured the left external ear from the top to the bottom with a transparent ruler. The result, together with the patient's age, was recorded. The ears ranged from 2.05 inches to 3.31 inches with a mean ear length of 2.66 inches. Based on study results, it would seem that as we get older our ears do indeed get bigger (by about 0.0087 of an inch per year).

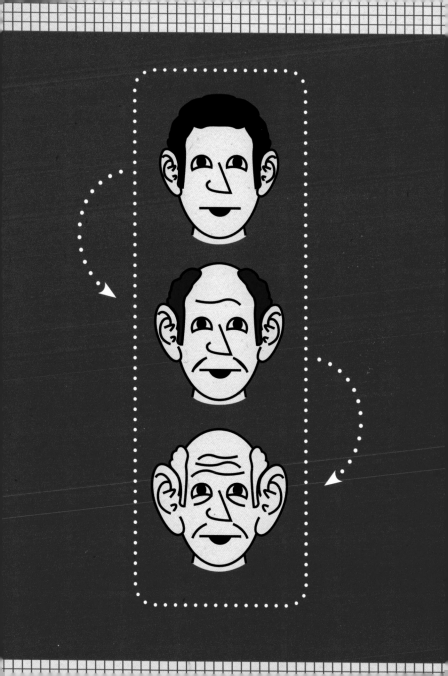

HOW MANY AMEND-MENTS HAVE THERE BEEN TO THE U.S. CONSTITUTION AND WHAT ARE THEY?

There are currently twenty-seven articles of amendment to the U.S. Constitution. The first ten were ratified collectively on December 15, 1791, and are known as the Bill of Rights. The most recent (and also the oldest) amendment was ratified in May 1992.

The amendments are:

Amendment 1 - Freedom of Religion, Press, Expression

Amendment 2 - Right to Bear Arms

Amendment 3 - Quartering of Soldiers

Amendment 4 - Search and Seizure

Amendment 5 - Trial and Punishment, Compensation for Takings

Amendment 6 - Right to Speedy Trial, Confrontation of Witnesses

Amendment 7 - Trial by Jury in Civil Cases

Amendment 8 - Cruel and Unusual Punishment

Amendment 9 - Construction of Constitution

Amendment 10 - Powers of the States and People

Amendment 11 - Judicial Limits

Amendment 12 - Choosing the President, Vice President

Amendment 13 - Slavery Abolished

Amendment 14 - Citizenship Rights

Amendment 15 - Race No Bar to Vote

Amendment 16 - Status of Income Tax Clarified

Amendment 17 - Senators Elected by Popular Vote
Amendment 18 - Liquor Abolished
Amendment 19 - Women's Suffrage
Amendment 20 - Presidential, Congressional Terms
Amendment 21 - Amendment 18 Repealed
Amendment 22 - Presidential Term Limits
Amendment 23 - Presidential Vote for District of Columbia
Amendment 24 - Poll Taxes Barred
Amendment 25 - Presidential Disability and Succession
Amendment 26 - Voting Age Set to 18 Years
Amendment 27 - Limiting Congressional Pay Increases

The Bill of Rights originally contained twelve proposed amendments, two of which failed to be ratified. The 27th Amendment was one of those that failed, but it was ratified more than 200 years later. The original first proposed amendment, the "Congressional Apportionment Amendment," has never been ratified.

Five other proposed amendments have been approved by Congress but have failed to be ratified by the requisite number of states' legislatures. Four are still technically pending, including the Corwin Amendment proposed in March 1861 for the preservation of slavery.

WHAT ARE THE ORIGINS OF THE HAMBURGER?

We will probably never know who first sold a beef patty stuck inside a bun, but there are lots of contenders for having invented something similar.

Genghis Khan and his army of ferocious Mongol horsemen used to snack on raw beef which they kept underneath their saddles; this tenderized the meat so that it could be eaten raw, and on the go. They also ground meat from lamb or mutton scrapings into patties. This was fast food for busy warriors intent on building the largest contiguous empire in history. When the Mongols invaded Russia, the snack became known as "Steak Tartare" (Tartar was the Russian name for the Mongols).

Minced beef was a delicacy in fifteenth-century Europe. In the seventeenth and eighteenth centuries trade between Germany and Russia gave rise to the "tartare steak," while the "Hamburg steak" became popular with German sailors along the New York City harbor. The latter was more likely salt beef: hard salted minced beef mixed with onions and breadcrumbs.

It's speculated that the first "Hamburger steak" was served at Delmonico's Restaurant in New York City in 1834, but not in a bun. In 1885 Charlie "Hamburger" Nagreen served flattened meatballs between two slices of bread at the Outgamie County Fair in Seymour, Wisconsin. As late as 1904 Fletcher Davis of Athens, Texas, attracted much media attention when he sold his hamburgers at the St. Louis World's Fair, again

on bread rather than a bun. Davis's claim to having originated the hamburger has been endorsed by both McDonalds and Dairy Queen. In 1980 DQ even ran a commercial filmed in Athens which referenced Davis's invention.

Brothers Frank and Charles Menches may also have made a major contribution to hamburger history: they sold ground pork sandwiches at the Erie Country Fair in New York, but one day in 1885, they were forced to use chopped beef because their butcher had run out of pork. They mixed in some coffee and brown sugar to "beef" up the taste and sold their "Hamburger Sandwiches." The name "Hamburger" came from Hamburg, New York, the location of the fair.

Lionel C. Sternberger is believed to have created the cheeseburger some time between 1924 and 1926 on Colorado Boulevard, in Pasadena.

IS IT POSSIBLE TO CONTROL YOUR DREAMS?

Yes. The technique is called "lucid dreaming," a term invented by Dutch psychiatrist Frederik van Eeden in his 1913 article "A Study of Dreams." Many people have reported lucid dreaming, or becoming aware that they are dreaming while still dreaming. Armed with this knowledge they can often influence events within the dream, and act out fantasies or consciously influence their subconscious.

Lucid dreaming has been popular since the 1960s, but the earliest written reference to controlling dreams occurs in in a letter written by St. Augustine of Hippo in A.D. 415. In the eighth century Tibetan Buddhists first practiced dream yoga to maintain waking consciousness while in a dream state.

There are several ways of inducing and prolonging a lucid dream state. Since lucid dreaming usually occurs when the dreamer spots something which wouldn't occur in waking life, performing reality testing while awake is a good way to train. To do this, try putting your finger through the palm of your hand, or holding your nose and trying to breathe with your mouth closed. This increases the chance of remembering to perform one of these reality tests while asleep, and recognizing the significance of the outcome.

Another step to lucid dreaming is remembering your dreams. Improving recall improves awareness of dreaming in general. You can write down what happens in your dreams, or speak about them into an audio recorder. Since staying still improves dream recall, dictation is a good method to use.

The most common technique to achieve lucid dreaming is Mnemonic Induction of Lucid Dreams (MILD). The technique was developed by Dr. Stephen LaBerge, a psychophysiologist and a leader in the scientific study of lucid dreaming. MILD involves focusing on a strong intention to dream lucidly while falling asleep and to commit to spotting signs that one is dreaming. After waking from a dream, if you can recall objects or events within the dream that would only happen in a dream, then there's a good chance you can go back to sleep and restart the dream in the same place, lucidly.

An extended version of this method is Wake-Back-to-Bed (WBTB) which involves sleeping for five to six hours, then waking up and staying awake for an hour while focusing on the subject of lucid dreaming (e.g., by reading a book about it), then going back to sleep while practicing the MILD method.

Lucid dreaming has been shown to help nightmare sufferers and has been used to treat depression.

HOW MANY PINTS OF BLOOD CAN I DONATE IN ONE SHOT WITHOUT DYING?

Most people have about 12 pints (4 liters) of blood. If you lose 4 pints quickly (i.e., by severing an artery) you will probably die. You can donate 3 pints over a period of several hours and survive, although you would be very weak, dehydrated, and in danger of life-threatening complications. You could safely donate 2 pints without harm, although it is not advisable. One pint remains the optimum amount to donate in a single sitting.

The American College of Surgeons' manual *Advanced Trauma Life Support* classifies hemorrhage and blood loss into four stages:

Class 1 Hemorrhage occurs when a person has lost up to 15 percent of his or her blood; this typically causes no change in vital signs.

Class 2 Hemorrhage involves losing between 15 and 30 percent of blood volume. The heart beats rapidly (a phenomenon known as tachycardia) and the blood vessels constrict to compensate for the drop in blood pressure and oxygenation. The skin turns pale, as oxygen levels are reduced. It is possible to survive this level of blood loss without a transfusion, but you will need a saline drip to replace the fluid volume.

Class 3 Hemorrhage occurs when there is a loss of between 30 and 40 percent of blood volume. The blood pressure drops dangerously low, the heart rate increases even more (putting great strain on the heart), and the subject becomes confused. Without intravenous fluids and blood transfusions, death is very likely.

Class 4 Hemorrhage involves the loss of more than 40 percent of circulating blood volume. This is right at the edge of what the human body can survive. Loss of more than 50 percent of circulating almost certainly will result in death.

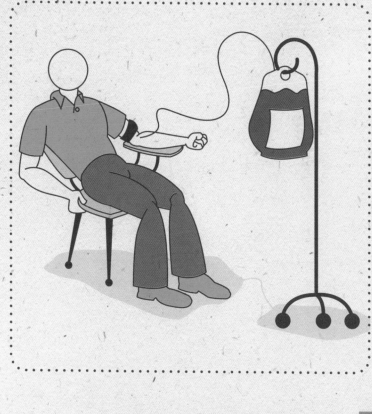

IS IT TRUE THAT ELEPHANTS NEVER FORGET?

The saying "an elephant never forgets" first appeared in print in 1904, when the *New York Times* reported a speech given by a trainer at the Ringling Brothers Circus. Since then, several scientific studies have recorded the true extent of a pachyderm's memory.

In the 1950s the German zoologist Bernhard Rensch investigated the relationship between brain size and intelligence. During his studies he experimented with a five-year-old Indian elephant. He presented the animal with two boxes: an empty one bearing the symbol of a circle on the lid, and one containing food marked by a cross. After more than 300 attempts the elephant finally twigged and thereafter consistently chose the box that contained the food. Rensch introduced further pairs of boxes marked with symbols, and the elephant was able to learn twenty different pairs and locate the food correctly nearly 600 times in a row.

In 1964 Leslie Squier taught three elephants to find sugar cubes by distinguishing between lights of different colors. Eight years later one of the animals remembered correctly; the other two were less successful but by then they were both nearly blind.

Dominant female elephants build up a social memory as they get older, which allows them to distinguish between friends and

outsiders. When the matriarchs encounter individuals they do not recognize, family members group together to protect their young. But they don't rely on sight alone; they can also distinguish between friends and strangers by smell or sound.

Elephants travel long distances to find food and water, and being able to remember favorable locations is vital for survival. This was highlighted in a 1993 study of three groups of elephants in Tanzania's Tarangire National Park during a severe drought. Two groups headed by matriarchs aged thirty-eight and forty-five left the park to find water, while the other group, led by a matriarch who was only thirty-three, stayed behind and suffered 63 percent of deaths in all three groups that year. The two older females had survived a comparable drought thirty-five years earlier; the younger female was unable to draw on this experience to save her family.

HOW CAN I JOIN THE MILE HIGH CLUB?

All that is required to join the Mile High Club is a willing partner over the age of consent (let's say over 21 to be on the safe side, as when you're in the air the laws of your state/country do not apply unless you happen to be flying over it at the time), an airline ticket, the self-control to be able to contain yourselves until the plane has reached at least a mile in altitude (that's about 5,280 feet), and the discretion to ensure that you don't get arrested for gross indecency.

That's it. No form filling, membership subscription, club magazines or dress code. Being a member of the Mile High Club may have a caché superior to that of your local golf club, but if you thought that there was any more to it than getting physical in the air, you are sorely mistaken. The MHC is merely a slang term for sex on an airplane, and membership is only a matter for personal testimonial.

The founding member of the club is considered to be a pilot and design engineer named Lawrence Sperry. He supposedly launched the idea by switching his plane to the newly-designed autopilot and getting busy with one Mrs. Waldo Polk during a flight on a Curtiss Flying Boat to New York in November 1916. Richard Branson, the owner of Virgin Atlantic Airways, claims to have joined the club when he was nineteen by having sex in the lavatory with a woman whom he later discovered was married.

The legality of having sex on a plane remains a gray area. If the act is performed in sight of others, it is illegal, but for international

flights the law varies according to the countries of departure and destination, the country the plane is flying over, and the nationality of the airline. The safest way to join is to book one of the many charter flights that cater specifically to this niche in the aviation market.

WHAT ARE HIDDEN MICKEYS?

The original Hidden Mickey was the silhouette of the head and ears of Mickey Mouse (one large circle, with two smaller circles on top). Scores of them are hidden in nearly all of Disney's animated classic movies as well as in many of their more recent movies. They're also plentiful among the architecture and attractions in Disney theme parks and studio buildings. The term has now been extended to describe any hidden representation of any part of Mickey Mouse, such as his white gloves or his clumpy yellow shoes, or other Disney characters (Hidden Minnies, Donald Ducks, Goofys, etc.), rather than a simple silhouette of Mickey's head.

The Walt Disney Company has never published a list of all the Hidden Mickeys. Even though they appear in Disney animated classics, the first recorded sighting wasn't made until 1989 when Arlen Miller wrote an article on them for Walt Disney World's *Eyes and Ears*. Since then the hunt for them has gone global. Several websites exist to document these sightings, many of which are wishful thinking; it's easy to spot three circles together if you look hard enough, but it doesn't mean you've found a Hidden Mickey.

The best book on the subject is the third edition of *Hidden Mickeys: A Field Guide to Walt Disney World's Best-Kept Secrets* by Steven M. Barrett.

Here are ten classic examples of Hidden Mickeys in Disney movies, but there are hundreds more:

1. *Sleeping Beauty* (1959): Near the beginning Merryweather says "I'd like to turn her into an old toad." A Hidden Mickey is carved into the green bench.

2. *Mary Poppins* (1964): Mickey's profile appears on the side of Bert's one-man-band drum.

3. *Aristocats* (1970): In the scene where the butler Edgar fights with the alley cats, there is a Hidden Mickey on the stone floor of the barn.

4. *Tron* (1982): As the heroes escape on the solar sailer a left-facing Mickey silhouette with open mouth and button nose can be clearly seen for a split second on the ground below.

5. *Lion King* (1994): When Scar is about to sing "Be Prepared" there is a profile of a Hidden Mickey in the third puff of green smoke.

6. *Toy Story* (1995): In Sid's room a rocker named "Mega Dork" depicted on a wall poster has a Mickey Mouse tattoo.

7. *The Hunchback of Notre Dame* (1996): In the opening sequence, as the camera pans over the city, Mickey's head appears on a rooftop and a sorcerer Mickey hat can be seen near the steeple.

8. *Monsters, Inc.* (2001): There is a child's drawing of Mickey Mouse on the drawing board in Boo's bedroom.

9. *Lilo and Stitch* (2002): In the opening scene scientist Jumba Jookiba stands on trial in a capsule. On the lower left of the capsule, a golden button becomes a Hidden Mickey for a few seconds.

10. *Pirates of the Caribbean: At World's End* (2007): Mickey Mouse appears on Sao Feng's navigational charts.

WHY IS THE *MONA LISA* SO FAMOUS AND VALUABLE?

Genius though he was, Leonardo da Vinci didn't produce many paintings because he was a perfectionist and spent years on each one. Only seventeen of them survive, and they are all very valuable. Leonardo began painting the *Mona Lisa* in 1503 and finished it shortly before his death in 1519. Today many consider it the most famous painting in the world, and one of the most precious, but this hasn't always been the case.

Upon his death, Leonardo bequeathed the painting to his assistant, Salai. During the 1530s it was displayed in a semi-public art gallery at Fontainebleau. In 1800 Napoleon hung it in his bedroom at the Tuileries Palace in Paris. It moved to the Louvre Museum four years later.

The *Mona Lisa* didn't become well-known until the Symbolist movement in the mid-nineteenth century, when it was viewed as the embodiment of eternal femininity. The painting's fame skyrocketed in the twentieth century, when it was stolen from the Louvre in 1911. The theft closed the museum down for a week. Pablo Picasso was one of the suspects, but it turned out the painting had been taken by a Louvre employee, Vincenzo Peruggia, who was apprehended two years later when he tried to sell it to the Uffizi Gallery in Florence.

Many things contribute to the painting's status: its unique and revolutionary aesthetics (the painting was the first to place its subject in front of a fantasy landscape); its mastery of realism against a fairytale background; the enigmat-

ic expression (the hint of the smile that has kept people guessing for 500 years); the overall harmony of composition; and the feeling of calm characteristic of all of Leonardo's work. Perhaps the most important element of the painting is the gaze: it meets ours, while Mona Lisa's posture and the visual impression of distance between sitter and observer that Leonardo created give her an almost divine inaccessibility.

Mona Lisa is a realistic woman and an ideal at the same time, full of contradictions. Dynamism, and a sense of movement, are always hailed as hallmarks of a masterpiece, and Leonardo succeeds in capturing dynamism in motion, rather than someone holding a half smile. Complex paintings evoke complex responses—there are no easy analyses or interpretations. The painting continually toys with our perceptions and emotions.

Speculation about the identity of the sitter also contributed to the painting's fame, until 2005 when a library expert at the University of Heidelberg discovered a 1503 margin note written by Agostini Vespucci. The sitter is now confirmed as Lisa del Giocondo, the wife of Francesco del Giocondo, a wealthy Florentine silk merchant. The painting was commissioned to celebrate the birth of their second child. Detailed analysis of the painting has shown that she is wearing a transparent gauze called a guarnello, typically worn by women while pregnant or after giving birth. Before then there had been much speculation about the woman's identity, including the suggestion that the painting was meant as an ironic self-portrait.

Above all, it is the enigmatic smile that continues to hold the public imagination in both popular culture and the art world. It is a smile that seems to disappear when you look at it directly and Leonardo painted with this intention. Professor Margaret Livingstone at Harvard University explains that "her smile is almost entirely in low spatial frequencies, and so is best seen by your peripheral vision," and says that artists like Leonardo "discovered fundamental truths that scientists are only now unraveling."

WHAT HAPPENED TO EINSTEIN'S BRAIN AFTER HE DIED?

On April 18, 1955, at 1:15 a.m., Albert Einstein died at the age of seventy-six from an aortic aneurysm the size of a small grapefruit. According to his wishes his body was cremated ("so people don't come to worship at my bones"), but not before a pathologist at Princeton Hospital, Dr. Thomas S. Harvey, performed an autopsy, during which he removed Einstein's brain and had it laminated.

Harvey preserved the brain in a 10 percent solution of formalin, then he photographed it from many angles, cut it into 240 slices, and sealed each one in celloidin. Originally, it was thought that the brain was removed with its owner's blessing but it is more likely that Einstein did not give his permission, and that his son, Hans Albert, only gave consent retrospectively. However, for Harvey, the opportunity to study the brain of one of the foremost geniuses of the twentieth century was a no-brainer: "To me it was obvious that the brain of this man should be studied. Here was

the brain of a genius—I thought, 'I better do a good job.'" His initial impression was that "It looked like any other brain."

For more than two decades nobody heard much more about Einstein's brain until 1978 when Stephen Levy, a curious young reporter working for the *New Jersey Monthly*, was ordered by his boss to track it down. Levy discovered that the brain was still in Harvey's care, although the doctor was now retired and living in Wichita, Kansas. The brain sections were preserved in alcohol in two large

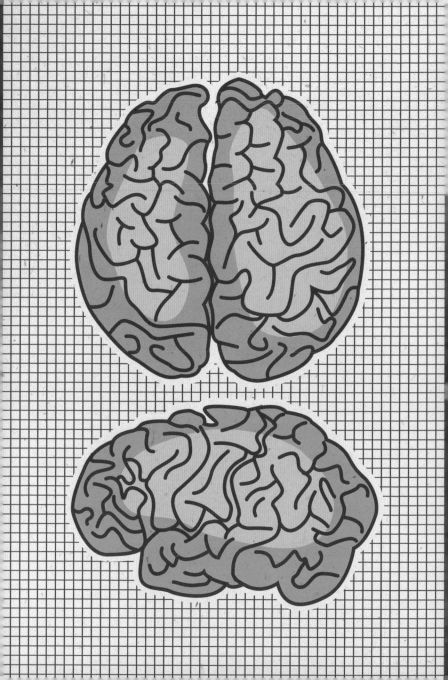

mason jars inside a box labeled "Costa Cider."

Since then, several scientific studies have been published about Einstein's brain. A 1985 article in *Experimental Neurology* entitled "On the brain of a scientist: Albert Einstein" focused on the ratio of neurons to glial cells (specialist cells that give the brain energy) and found that in the left side of his brain there were 73 percent more glial cells than average. Although these findings might suggest that Einstein's neurons were unusually energy-hungry, it may have simply been the case that he was using his brain more than most. The study didn't compare like with like, however—the other brains were from younger subjects, with an average age of sixty-four—so maybe the findings were age- rather than genius-related.

An article published in 1996 in *Neuroscience Letters* entitled "Alterations in cortical thickness and neuronal density in the frontal cortex of Albert Einstein" suggested that Einstein's brain may have had a denser concentration of neurons because his cerebral cortex was thinner than average. That same year the *Lancet* published "The exceptional brain of Albert Einstein" which posited that a series of unique grooves on an area of the brain associated with math and spatial reasoning may have allowed his neurons to communicate better with each other. Three years later a McMaster University study of Dr. Harvey's photographs disclosed that Einstein's brain had a truncated Sylvian fissure (the line dividing the frontal lobe and parietal lobe from the temporal lobe). Researchers speculated that this too may have improved neuron communication in that area.

In 1998, Thomas Harvey finally parted with his two jars, and handed what was left of Einstein's gray matter to the Princeton Medical Center, where it remains today.

COULD I SURVIVE A FALL FROM AN AIRPLANE WITHOUT A PARACHUTE?

The short answer is yes, but the odds are stacked against you. When you jump out of an airplane, your body inevitably starts plunging downwards and continues to accelerate until it reaches terminal velocity, which is about 125 mph if your arms and legs are fully extended. If you curl into a ball or fall straight like an arrow, your terminal velocity will be closer to 200 mph. To increase your chances of survival, you should keep your speed as low as possible by adopting the classic starfish skydiver body shape.

Terminal velocity is one of the reasons why it is possible to survive a fall without a parachute. If it weren't for the air molecules colliding with your falling body and creating an upward force, opposing gravity, you would continue to accelerate. This would mean that at the point of impact with the ground, your speed would be so great that even with the best luck in the world, the physical forces exerted on your body would be impossible to survive.

Before you get too excited, though, it is worth remembering that the majority of people who free-fall without a parachute are toast. There are several documented cases, however, of people surviving, sometimes with minimal injuries:

• In 1963 U.S. Marine pilot Cliff Judkin bailed out of his crippled fighter plane. When his parachute failed to open, he plunged 15,000 feet into the Pacific Ocean. Judkin suffered numerous broken bones and a collapsed lung, but he survived the fall.

• In 1943 U.S. Army air force sergeant Alan Magee fell 20,000 feet after bailing out of a burning B-17 and broke his fall by crashing through a skylight of a French train station. He survived, albeit with a shattered arm.

• The most remarkable case is that of RAF flight sergeant Nicholas Alkemade who jumped from a Lancaster bomber at 18,000 feet and 90 seconds later crashed through pine trees to land in snow. His worst injuries were burns sustained in the aircraft before he jumped.

Short of growing feathers in midair, it would seem the best way to improve your chances of survival is to limit your terminal velocity and find some way of gradually breaking your fall.

IS IT POSSIBLE TO BECOME A MILLIONAIRE WITHOUT BEING SELFISH?

Every day a mind-boggling number of people type the phrases "make money fast," "become a millionaire," or "get rich quick" into Internet search engines. Everyone wants to live the dream, but many of us suspect that being nice just doesn't cut it when you're trying to hack off a big fat slice of the fiscal pie for yourself. But do you have to tread on other people to become a millionaire?

The principles of wealth creation do not depend on taking advantage of other people. In fact, the greatest entrepreneurs know that they have to help other people in order to help themselves, because nobody gets rich on his or her own. Here are five simple rules that will help you to become rich, without railroading everyone else in the process:

1. Follow your heart. Most millionaires spend their lives doing something that would give them lots of job satisfaction even if it didn't earn them lots of money. For example, as a teenager Bill Gates went into software because he loved tinkering around with computers. He followed his passion, and just happened to be a very shrewd and strategic businessman along the way. Ask the world's richest people and they'll likely say they're in it for the "game" rather than the money.

2. Learn to recognize the difference between assets and liabilities. Assets generate money, while

liabilities cost money. Instead of buying a new sports car (which is a liability), use that money to create an asset (an investment or a company, for example) that will generate the money to pay for the car. Then you'll have the car, plus the asset, which continues to generate more income.

3. Be a super saver rather than a super spender and start saving early. A savings plan opened in your late teens and early twenties will grow considerably larger than one started just five years later.

4. Do less but do it well, rather than trying to do it all.

5. Ask yourself what kind of education and communication skills you'll need to become a millionaire, then go out and get them. Consider what sort of people you should be associating with and seeking advice from, then find and befriend them. Decide what goals you need to set and follow them. Ask yourself what you will have to become in order to become a millionaire. While you are concentrating on developing all these skills, you may make many millions, but the self-development will be more valuable than all your wealth.

WHAT CAUSES CAR SICKNESS?

Car sickness is a form of motion sickness, or kinetosis, that occurs when the brain receives conflicting messages from the body (including the inner ear, eyes, and muscles). The fluid in your inner ear responds to motion and your orientation in space while your eyes also send your brain messages about your environment. Reading a book while traveling often leads to nausea because the eyes are staring at a stationary page while the fluid in the inner ear registers movement. The brain interprets this conflict to mean that the body is impaired by some form of ingested poison, so it makes you sick to flush out the perceived toxin.

One of the best ways to alleviate car sickness is to stare toward the horizon in the direction of travel. This gives the brain visual motion cues that correspond with those of the inner ear.

Children, especially those between the ages of three and twelve, are more prone to car sickness than adults, probably because they are less likely to sit still and they are usually in the back, while the adults in the front get to stare at the horizon. Women are twice as likely to be affected as men.

Car sickness may be on the decline today, with fewer incidents than there were thirty years ago. What's so different today? For starters, the greater number of highways means steadier driving and less twisting around on old roads, a contributing factor to motion sickness. Maybe the biggest change is improved vehicle suspension, although more people are driving pick-up trucks than ever before, and those don't exactly win awards for their silky-smooth ride.

DO INSECTS SLEEP?

Yes, but not in the same way that humans do. Given that the physiology of insects is very different from ours, insect biologists are reluctant to call periods of rest and inactivity in their subjects "sleep"; instead they use the term "torpor." While the process of torpor is very different from sleep, for all intents and purposes, it is fair to say insects do sleep in that they undergo periods where they are not fully awake.

According to the *American Heritage Dictionary*, sleep can be defined as "a natural periodic state of rest for the mind and body, in which the eyes usually close and consciousness is completely or partially lost, so that there is a decrease in bodily movement and responsiveness to external stimuli."

Many insects go into a period of torpor, where they show a greatly reduced response to stimuli. The length and depth of torpor differs greatly between insect species. Some insects have a very short lifespan so they don't waste their time in torpor. It's very difficult to measure the slowing down of physiological processes in insects, and no one has yet managed to measure insect brain activity. Some, like the New Zealand weta, a large flightless cricket that lives at high altitude, freeze solid at night and thaw out in the morning. Others have been observed to slow down in low temperatures (and many hibernate). Insects that are active during the day become inactive at night, but many simply appear to be more lethargic than down for the count.

Migrating Monarch butterflies gather together and rest at night. Flies, beetles, and cockroaches all have rest periods. Ants go

into torpor, but there always appears to be activity in an ant's nest because they work and rest in shifts. At sundown some species of bee bite on a leaf, fold their legs up, and dangle lifelessly all night by their jaws; many return to the same place every evening.

Other insects play possum, faking death to evade a predator. These include most caterpillars, which curl up into a ball when disturbed, and many beetles, which rest on their backs with their legs folded into their bodies. These episodes can last anywhere from a few minutes to several hours.

One thing insects don't do when they "sleep" is close their eyes. Why? Because they don't have eyelids.

WHY ARE CORPSES BURIED "SIX FEET UNDER"?

They aren't—or at least, they don't have to be. There was no set depth for burial on record until the outbreak of the plague in London in 1665 which, according to Daniel Defoe's fictional account, *A Journal of the Plague Year*, prompted the Lord Mayor of London to order several actions in the interests of public health. Among these were that the dead should be buried either before sunrise or after sunset, and to a depth of at least six feet. It was hoped that this would halt the spread of disease from dead bodies, although the measure had little impact since the plague was actually spread by fleas.

A tangible benefit of a deep grave is that it deters scavengers, both animal and human. Because grave robbing has been a problem since before the Egyptians built the pyramids, the security provided by a deep grave is self-evident. Prior to 1665, shallow graves often resulted in graveyards being littered with bones and decaying flesh.

Within a few decades after the plague outbreak British burial requirements became much more lax. Today, the minimum requirements for burial, as set out in by the government in 1977, is at least three feet of soil above the coffin. In the United States, there has never been a minimum depth requirement of six feet. In California, caskets must be buried beneath at least eighteen inches of soil. In practice burial depth varies from as little as eighteen inches to twelve feet. In low-lying areas, the deeper the grave the better its chances of becoming waterlogged, and the soil above a coffin is usually no more than two feet deep. In the city of New Orleans, which is below sea level, many coffins are buried above ground in mausoleums.

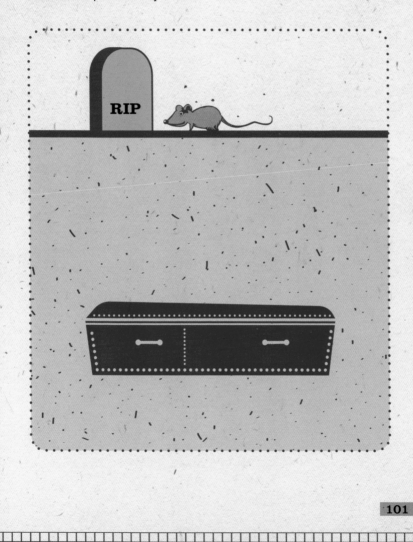

ARE THERE ANY TRUE STORIES OF PEOPLE WAKING UP WITH KIDNEYS MISSING?

The victim in the many versions of this classic urban myth usually gets slipped a mickey while talking to a beautiful stranger in a bar, and wakes up later lying in a bath filled with ice and a note urging him to seek urgent medical attention.

First, let's consider the feasibility of kidney theft as a way of earning a dishonest living because, let's face it, there are plenty of crimes that don't involve intricate surgical procedures. Another downside: kidneys don't have the same shelf life as Class A drugs or fake designer purses, and matching them is a difficult business that requires access to a victim's medical records. Frankly, it all sounds like too much bother.

So where did the story come from? Well, the source of the legend probably began with a Reuters wire report dated December 8, 1989, in which a thirty-four-year-old Turkish man, Ahmet Koc, claimed to have arrived in Britain in 1988 on the promise of work, whereupon he was brought to a hotel where his kidney was removed against his will and transplanted into another patient.

The kidney removal did take place, but contrary to his claims, Koc had been a willing participant; it turns out he had placed an ad in a Turkish newspaper offering to sell one of his kidneys. He concocted the theft story the following year to avoid a prison sentence while giving evidence to a General

Medical Council hearing against the doctors who performed the procedure.

A 1991 episode of the TV show *Law and Order* entitled "Sonata for Solo Organ" featured organ theft, drawing its inspiration from Koc's story, further fueling the fledgling urban legend in which the victim was discovered in a blood-soaked bed, or propped against a building. A few years later versions of the legend changed to the victim waking up in a bathtub full of ice. Since then the organ theft has been reported as occurring in Las Vegas, Texas, and Louisiana, and the victims have been a student, an administrative assistant, and an adulterous husband getting his just desserts.

It's an impressive track record for a tale that began twenty years ago as a Koc-and-bull story.

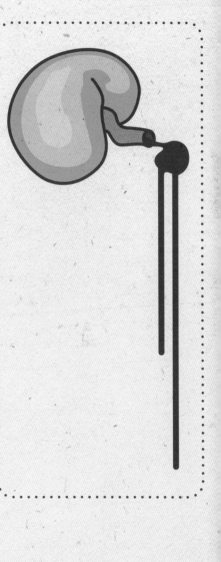

WHAT IS A UVULA FOR?

The uvula is the little blob of tissue that hangs down at the back of your throat. Most people are barely aware that it's there and are only reminded of its existence while watching cartoon characters with acrobatic uvulas sing at the top of their lungs or scream in excruciating pain. But what does the uvula actually do?

Quite a lot, as it turns out. It plays an important role in speech production, even in English. Try this: slowly say the consonant "m" followed by the consonant "b." Both sounds use exactly the same process of articulation with one crucial difference: for the "m," the uvula remains in a lowered position allowing air to pass into the nose; for the "b," the uvula and soft palate press upwards against the back of the throat and close off the air to the nasal passage. You should be able to feel a build-up of air at the back of your throat just before you release it to say "b": if it didn't release you would sound very nasal. People with very small uvulas (a condition called "velopharyngeal insufficiency," or VPI) can't say "b"—it comes out as "m" instead.

The uvula is also essential in other languages to make certain guttural sounds (such as the rolled "r" in French). Arabic languages, Hebrew, and many African languages couldn't do without it either.

The purpose of the uvula isn't merely for pronunciation's sake. Whenever you swallow, the soft palate and the uvula move upward to close off the nasopharynx so that you don't get food up your nose. Sometimes this mechanism malfunctions, as you may have discovered if someone has ever made you laugh while you are drinking. The laughter makes your palate and uvula drop down, allowing the drink to spurt out of your nose.

The uvula plays a big part in snoring. An elongated or swollen uvula partially obstructs the passage of air between the lungs and the mouth, and the resulting vibration causes the snoring sound. Sleep apnea occurs when the passage of air is completely blocked and the sufferer wakes up scores of times each night. If snoring is extreme, the reduction or removal of the uvula is an option, but the success rate is relatively low (about 40 percent).

WHAT WOULD HAPPEN IF EVERYONE IN CHINA JUMPED IN THE AIR AT THE SAME TIME?

Not a lot, despite a plethora of theories and urban myths surrounding the catastrophic results of such coordinated mass action—from a tidal wave that would engulf the rest of the world to the Earth being knocked out of its rotational orbit.

Earth has a mass of approximately 6×10^{21} tons. There are approximately 1.3 billion people in China, and their combined weight would be a tiny fraction of the mass of the Earth.

Imagine a giant ball the size of a football stadium. Now suppose that a billion ants are gathered somewhere on its surface and they all decide to jump in the air at the same time. Do you think it would have any significant impact on the ball? The same principle applies to humans jumping on the Earth.

Besides, the Earth and everything on it is a closed system. As long as people don't reach escape velocity (the speed sufficient to overcome Earth's gravity) there will be no noticeable effect when they all jump.

A really interesting question is just how much money and organization it would take to get the whole population of China to jump at the same time. It would require thousands of synchronized clocks, and the whole economy would grind to a halt for several days to allow for the mass migration of people to jump in time zones spread out around the country.

What if everyone on the planet (over 6 billion of us) jumped at the same time? It would be impossible to coordinate, of course, but let's imagine for a moment that we have solved that little logistical problem and that everyone from New York cab drivers to the Bushmen of the Kalahari basin is taking part. What then? Still not much. Makes you feel kind of insignificant, doesn't it?

WHY DO HUMANS KISS?

You might consider the answer to this question to be self-evident: because it feels nice. So nice, in fact, that the average person is said to spend about two weeks kissing over his or her lifetime. But humans don't just lock lips for fun. At least that's what philematologists (those who formally study anatomy and the evolutionary history of kissing) argue.

The big debate about smooching is whether the behavior is learned or instinctive. Those who argue the former point out that kissing is not found in all human cultures, and that about 10 percent of humans don't do it. For example, in Thailand they don't kiss—they sniff each other's cheeks. The Chewa and Thonga tribes of Africa are reported to have been repulsed when they saw Europeans kiss and assumed that they were exchanging saliva. French kissing was fairly uncommon until after Victorian times.

Those who believe kissing is instinctive cite the many animals that show kissing-like behaviours. Chimpanzees, especially Bonobos, pucker up as a gesture of affection just as humans do; they even kiss and make up after a fight. In some cultures the word "to kiss" means to smell, so the act is more about the desire to smell a lover than to swap spit. Herein lies a clue to kissing's possible instinctive origins: smell is a primary component of pair bonding. The kiss enables us to get close and soak up each other's pheromones and perform a vital exchange of biological and genetic information when seeking out a mate. For example, it has been shown that women subcon-

sciously prefer the scent of men who have key immune system proteins different from their own. Also we mustn't forget that there are lots of nerve endings in the lips, and kissing releases endorphins into the brain that help to relieve stress and increase heart rate. In short, kissing is good for you—in more ways than one.

DO CELL PHONES CAUSE BRAIN CANCER?

The jury is still out on this one as studies continue to contradict one another. A link has been found between brain tumors and the old analogue mobile phones but brain tumors take a long time to develop, so it will be several years before scientists will be able to determine whether there are any harmful effects from the digital phones currently in use.

Let's begin by looking at the "radiation" involved with mobile phone use. All cell phones emit low levels of electromagnetic radiation. They operate with radio frequencies (RF) which lie on the electromagnetic spectrum between FM radio waves and microwaves. How much exposure is safe?

There are two basic types of radiation: ionizing and non-ionizing. Ionizing radiation such as Gamma rays and X-rays are powerful enough to strip atoms and molecules from DNA and affect chemical reactions inside the body. Exposure can cause serious tissue damage. Exposure to low levels of non-ionizing radiation such as radio-frequencies, visible light, and microwaves, however, is generally regarded as being safe in the short term; the long-term consequences of prolonged exposure have yet to be measured.

Exposure to high RF levels causes tissues to heat up, in much the same way that microwaves heat food; mobile phones operate at levels well below this. Individual exposure depends upon several factors, such as the distance from the transmitter, the duration of the call, and the angle at which the phone is held to the ear. Regardless, John E. Moulder, Professor of Radiation Oncology at the Medical college of Wisconsin, speaks for many radiation experts when he says that biological effects of cell phones are "somewhere between impossible and implausible."

A report published in the *European Journal of Cancer Prevention* has shown that people who used the old analogue cell phones for more than ten years are more than twice as likely to develop brain tumors. But several studies have shown that there is no link between brain cancer and digital mobile phone use, either in terms of the type of cancer or the side of the head on which the cancer occurred. Some studies have shown increased tumor development in laboratory rats that were pre-sensitized to develop cancer or that were exposed for at least 22 hours per day. The implications of these results on human health are not clear.

The current FDA position *is* clear: "The available scientific evidence does not demonstrate any adverse health effects associated with the use of mobile phones." Nevertheless, there is a vocal if small minority of experts who believe cell phones are quite dangerous. Neurosurgeon Dr. Vini Khurana warns people to avoid using cell phones where possible, and that governments must take "immediate steps" to deal with the public health risks. He says, "There is a significant and increasing body of evidence for a link between mobile phone usage and certain brain tumors" which he believes will be "definitely proven" in the near future. If he is right, then with worldwide cell phone usage at three billion people and rising, mobiles may prove to be the tobacco and asbestos of the twenty-first century.

DID COCA-COLA REALLY USED TO CONTAIN COCAINE?

The exact formula of Coca-Cola has always been a trade secret, but it was named for its two "medicinal" ingredients: extract of coca leaves (a source of cocaine) and kola nuts. Although the amounts of cocaine that ended up in Coca-Cola were very small, traces of it were present until 1929.

Coke was originally formulated in 1886 by John Pemberton, an Atlanta druggist and former Confederate army officer. Back then cocaine was legal and sold over the counter in a wide range of medicinal products from drinks to toothpaste. Coca-Cola was just another beverage being touted as a patent medicine. Pemberton described his product as "the greatest blessing to the human family, Nature's (God's) best gift in medicine" which would "cure all nervous afflictions" especially headaches and fatigue.

How much cocaine Coke actually contained is hard to determine, although many sources estimate that it contained 9 milligrams per glass (the average street dose today is 20-30 milligrams). For many years Coke was referred to by Southerners as "dope," soda fountains were called "hop joints," and Coke delivery trucks "dope wagons."

In the 1890s people wised up to the damaging qualities of cocaine, as increasing numbers were becoming addicted. Asa Candler, who had bought the infant Coke company from Pemberton, was initially reluctant to eliminate extract of coca leaves from his product because he considered that this would weaken his claim to exclusive use of the name Coca-Cola, as well as open his company up to lawsuits. His first priority was to protect the brand.

By 1929 cocaine was completely eliminated from Coca-Cola and today a cocaine-free coca leaf is used. Even so, the manufacturing plant in Maywood, New Jersey, is the only one authorized by the Federal Government to import and process the coca plant.

CAN ANIMALS BE GAY?

Homosexuality is a controversial topic amongst biologists, with many arguing that homosexual behavior in animals takes place under "unnatural" circumstances. Recent research, however, has shown that same-sex coupling occurs in a wide range of animals from giraffes to flamingos and salmon.

In his 1999 book *Biological Exuberance: Animal Homosexuality and Natural Diversity*, Bruce Bagemihl documents no fewer than 450 different vertebrate species which engage in same sex mating (University of Oslo zoologist Petter Böckman believes the figure is closer to 1,500), and presents compelling evidence that animals are not solely driven by heterosexual urges. Furthermore, he reveals bigotry in the biological sciences stretching back over 200 years of observations of animal behavior, including homosexuality. He argues that gay human beings are not alone in the animal kingdom, which enjoys multiple shades of sexual orientation.

Both male and female flamingos form homosexual relationships. Some male swans have sex with a female, and then chase her away after she has laid an egg, which he then raises with his male partner. Giraffes, killer whales, and West Indian manatees indulge in all-male orgies. A recent study of koalas in Australia found that homosexual encounters outnumbered heterosexual ones by three to one. Female Japanese macaques frequently mount each other, while between 40 and 50 percent of all bonobo sexual exchanges are homosexual. Female bonobos participate in lesbian sex several times a day.

Joan Roughgarden, a professor of biology at Stanford University, has cataloged a wealth of homosexual behavior in the animal kingdom and published the results in her book *Evolution's Rainbow*. She argues that homosexuality is an essential part of biology, and that not every sexual act requires a reproductive function: "The time has come to declare that sexual theory is indeed false and to stop shoe-horning one exception after another into a sexual selection framework . . . to do otherwise suggests that sexual selection theory is unfalsifiable, not subject to refutation." She counters the Darwinist argument that being gay is biologically futile because it does not pass on genes, by observing that if homosexuality were a harmful or maladaptive trait, it would have disappeared long ago. To the contrary, she argues, it must have been carefully preserved by natural selection. One benefit of same sex union in the animal kingdom is that childless individuals contribute to the gene pool by nurturing the young of others.

CAN YOU CATCH A SEXUALLY TRANSMITTED DISEASE FROM A TOILET SEAT?

There's only one sexually transmitted disease (STD) that you could conceivably catch from a toilet seat, albeit with great difficulty: pubic lice (crabs). You are more likely to catch crabs from other sources such as infected bedding, clothing, and cloth-covered furniture. Lice cannot survive away from the human body for more than 24 hours.

Many disease-causing organisms can't survive very long outside the host body (in some cases not more than a few seconds). Even if someone with an STD had been rubbing their infected genitals on the seat before you, and even if the germs did manage to somehow enter your body through your urethral or genital tract or on a cut or sore on your buttocks, there would still probably not be sufficient quantities to infect you.

Most STDs can only be transmitted through the genitals or from skin to skin during sexual contact (that's why they're called STDs). Many people incorrectly believe that catching Herpes from a toilet seat is a common occurrence. Herpes can cause fluid-filled lesions in the mouth or facial area (Herpes I) or on the genitals (Herpes type II). The fluid contains the virus, so if the lesions burst, Herpes can be spread by kissing or shaking hands. Scientists have established that Herpes II can remain infectious on toilet seats for two to four hours after contact and on dry gauze for up to seventy-two hours. So infection from an inanimate object such as a toilet seat, towel, or drinking vessel is theoretically possible, but there are no documented cases of the disease actually being spread in this way (although plenty of people like to use this excuse to cover their tracks after they have been unfaithful).

Abigail Salyers, Ph.D., the president of the American Society for Microbiology, should have the final word: "To my knowledge, no one has ever acquired an STD on the toilet seat, unless they were having sex on it."

DOES DRINKING SEA WATER MAKE YOU GO MAD?

The *Admiralty Manual of Seamanship* published by the British Royal Navy in 1964 advises that sea water is poisonous. According to the manual, "Numerous lives were lost from this cause during the last war. Madness and death follow very quickly after drinking sea water."

The truth is that drinking a small amount of clean sea water won't do you any harm, especially if you also drink plenty of fresh water to help your body flush out the sodium chloride. However, if you drink sea water exclusively for the purposes of hydration then you will quickly find yourself in trouble. If you continue to drink sea water and no other hydrating fluids, the sodium levels in your blood will rise to toxic levels, water will be expelled from the cells in your body, your nervous system will crash, and you will experience seizures, brain damage, and ultimately heart and kidney failure.

You will also become more thirsty, as your body uses more water than it takes in to flush out the salt. While you are still conscious, you will experience raging thirst, delirium, confusion, and an overwhelming fear that you are about to die. Mad or not, you certainly won't be very rational.

Fresh water has fewer than 1,000 parts per million (ppm) of dissolved salts. That means that less than 0.1 percent of the water's weight is salt. Human blood is around 0.9 percent and sea water is about 3.5 percent salt by weight.

Several ocean travelers have reported drinking a mixture of sea and fresh water with no ill effects. Norwegian explorer and writer Thor Heyerdahl reported drinking 40 percent sea water mixed with 60 percent fresh water during his 1947 expedition across the Pacific Ocean on board the raft *Kon-Tiki*. In 1952 "voluntary castaway" Dr. Alain Bombard spent 65 days on board a tiny inflatable, the *Heretique*, to prove that castaways could and should drink small quantities of sea water, while collecting fresh water from condensation. However, his findings are controversial and the maritime rule is still to avoid drinking sea water at all costs.

ARE THERE ALLIGATORS LIVING IN THE SEWERS OF NEW YORK CITY?

There used to be at least one, but there aren't anymore. The story has now become an urban legend, but it seems to have been based on truth.

On February 10, 1935, the *New York Times* reported that eight teenagers had discovered a seven-foot alligator while they were shoveling snow into an open manhole on East 123rd Street. They pulled the creature out of the sewer with a rope, and then beat it to death with their snow shovels after it snapped at them. At the time it was decided that the creature didn't live in the sewer, but had merely escaped from a boat up from the Everglades and then swum up the Harlem River and into a storm drain.

Twenty-four years later novelist Robert Daley published a book called *The World Beneath the City*, which recounts that the 1935 sighting was the first of many in that year which eventually led to a mass cull. The sewer workers had begun reporting sightings of smaller alligators—about two feet in length—in the sewer system. Their supervisor, Teddy May, reasoned "them guys been drinking in there" and he sprung into action to discover how they were smuggling whiskey down in the pipes. However, he claims that he soon witnessed a large number of alligators firsthand, and initiated a large-scale extermination effort by using poison and flushing the reptiles out of the smaller pipes where they were either shot or washed out to sea. Within a few months they were gone.

That should have been the end of the matter, but rumors of alligator sightings refused to subside. The existence of alligators in the sewers was widely attributed to families bringing tiny specimens back from vacation as pets, and then flushing them down the toilet when they became too big to manage. However, if they were too big to manage, how come they were still small enough to flush?

If pets were really given up this way, it is more likely that they were shoved down a manhole at night by tired parents.

Today all we can say with any certainty is that a seven-foot alligator was discovered in 1935 by snow shovelers. The rest can probably be attributed to the fertile imagination of Teddy May.

COULD I KNOCK OUT MIKE TYSON WITH A LUCKY PUNCH?

Online sources have referred to Mike Tyson as "basically a neck with legs and arms sticking out." If you are going to knock him out with a lucky punch, how many pounds per square inch (psi) would you have to generate? His 18 inches of solid neck muscles alone are going to absorb most of the impact.

History's top hitting fighters, among them George Foreman and Earnie Shavers, hit at about 1,600 psi. One of Tyson's punches, even now, has the potential to put the average man in the hospital. A knockout punch from Tyson stands a good chance of fracturing your skull, whereas you've probably got a less than 1 percent chance of doing him any damage. His punch is equivalent to getting hit by a 16-pound sledgehammer swung at 35 miles per hour or hitting a car windshield at 50 miles per hour, and he has taken many similar punches during his career.

Unless you are a boxer or mixed martial artist you won't even land a punch before Tyson knocks you out. If you did throw a jab, he would bob and weave, roll, or simply move his head to one side while keeping his center of gravity stable, making your shot glance harmlessly off his head, or miss completely. He always was a master at that, and it means that he could stay in range to deliver a devastating counterpunch that would put you on the canvas. In fact, what he'd probably do is take your shot and counter, so that you'd walk right into his fist while he protected his face with his bicep and forearm. Either way, you would be down within the first few seconds of the fight and leave the ring in an ambulance. If you've never had any boxing or martial arts training, there's a better chance that Tyson will pop an artery than succumb to whatever you can throw at him.

WHY ARE DOCTORS SO UNHEALTHY?

There are several reasons why the mental health of doctors is significantly worse than for many other profressions. Doctors have excessive workloads, long hours, poor management, a constant anxiety over complaints and possible litigation, and quite often inadequate resources—all of which causes a whole heap of stress. Add to this their frequent reluctance to seek help and their view that illness is a sign of weakness and you'll understand their high suicide rate—about 300 to 400 doctors kill themselves each year. Many thousands more suffer with undiagnosed depression, or have self-medicating or substance abuse issues.

The two greatest causes of work stress are a "demand-control imbalance" or an "effort-rewards imbalance." The former means that the job combines high demands and responsibility, while giving the worker little control over his or her environment or the factors that influence it. A recent survey of 608 physicians in the United States found that "sense of control over the practice environment" was the most important predictor of well-being and good mental health. However, doctors are not at the heart of the administrative decision-making process, and often feel a lack of control. The latter means that the worker perceives the rewards for his or her work as disproportionately low compared to the effort required. Both of these conditions apply to doctors. They play an insufficient role in the design and delivery of healthcare, and while they are paid well, they often receive neither praise nor the satisfaction of a job well done, especially since mistakes can lead to litigation.

Doctors' personalities may also contribute to their suffering in silence. As a group they are perfectionists, approval-seeking, and overly conscientious. They have a strong need to be in control, which is what makes them good at their job, but these traits don't necessarily contribute to high self-esteem or good mental health when they manifest as inflexibility, overcommitment to work, and the inability to switch off.

Doctors feel that their first responsibility is to their patients. The Brown Medical School mission statement says: "We intend that our students follow in the altruistic tradition of medicine, placing the welfare of their patients and society above self-interest." As a whole doctors are reluctant to seek help from within the medical profession, and are more likely to self-medicate or turn to drugs or alcohol to cope with their everyday stresses. Studies show that doctors are less likely than people in any other profession to take time off for being sick. There is a stigma attached to calling in sick, since this places an increased workload on others, and raises doubts about professional competence. Consequently, they keep minor issues hidden and untreated, which is why the most common reasons for early retirement amongst doctors are psychiatric: depression, anxiety, and alcoholism.

WHY DID ADOLF HITLER, A HIGH-SCHOOL DROPOUT, BECOME THE LEADER OF THE NAZI PARTY?

Adolf Hitler was born in Austria on April 20, 1889. Although he was the fourth child of six, only he and his younger sister Paula survived to adulthood. He had a turbulent and unhappy childhood, a deep emotional attachment to his mother, and hatred for his violent and abusive father.

Adolf's family moved several times during his childhood before settling in the city of Linz. Adolf was a good elementary school student but he had to repeat his first year at high school and his teachers observed that he had "no desire to work." He dropped out of school at age sixteen without any qualifications for work.

He spent the next few years at home with his mother, frustrated, directionless, and idle. She encouraged him to adopt a trade, but Adolf refused to submit to authority and the drudgery of work.

Instead he luxuriated in pseudo-gentlemanly pursuits: reading, drawing, and wandering around Linz visiting museums and the opera, all the while fantasizing about becoming a great artist. Adolf didn't have a girlfriend, although he did jealously obsess over a young lady called Stephanie, with whom he believed he could communicate telepathically while she remained oblivious to his feelings. His only companion at the time was August Kubizek, a young musician with similar dreams of artistic fame and fortune.

During this time Adolf devoured books on German history and Nordic mythology and began to formulate his ideas about German nationalism. He already had a deep enmity towards non-Germanic races and a belief in German superiority.

In October 1907, when he was eighteen, Adolf decided to follow his passion for drawing and architecture, and applied to the Vienna Academy of Fine Arts. He used his inheritance money to move to Vienna, leaving behind his mother who earlier in the year had undergone a mastectomy after being

diagnosed with breast cancer. Adolf failed the entrance exam, and was advised to pursue architecture, but he didn't have the grades to take it any further. He returned home, kept quiet about his failure, and spent the next few weeks nursing his mother until her death just before Christmas.

Inconsolable with grief, Adolf moved back to Vienna, determined to reapply to art school, but in October 1908 he once again failed the admission test to the Academy. Even his friend August Kubizek seemed to be moving on—he had been accepted into the Vienna Conservatory to study music, while Adolf became so poor he ended up eating at soup kitchens, burning with a fierce sense of injustice at his lot. Still, he refused to seek employment. In December 1909 he moved into a hostel for the homeless where he stayed for the next few years, continuing to study books on history and philosophy. While there his new obsessions became politics and anti-Semitism. In *Mein Kampf*, Hitler claimed that in Vienna he

"ceased to be a weak-kneed cosmopolitan and became an anti-Semite."

He left Vienna at the age of twenty-four to dodge the draft, but when World War I started he volunteered for the Bavarian Regiment and for the first time in his life discovered a new sense of belonging and purpose: "Compared to the events of this gigantic struggle, everything in my past receded to shallow nothingness."

Hitler became a dispatch runner in the trenches, one of the most dangerous jobs in the army, but despite being a sloppy soldier he volunteered for dangerous missions while demonstrating an uncanny knack for beating the odds. At Ypres, 80 percent of his regiment was killed or wounded, but Adolf remained unscathed until he was wounded in the leg during the Battle of the Somme on October 7, 1916. Following a few months of convalescence he volunteered to return to the front line, where he received the Iron Cross for bravery, although he was never promoted beyond the rank of Corporal because his superiors considered him poor leadership material. He was injured and stepped out again in October 1918, a month before the end of the war.

After Germany's defeat, convinced that the Fatherland had been betrayed by Jews and Marxists, Hitler the bitter war veteran channeled his ambitions and hatred into politics. The humiliating Treaty of Versailles forced Germany to take full responsibility for the war and crippled the country with reparations. This led to a growing wave of nationalism, on which Hitler spent the next decade surfing into power. First, he was an undercover agent in the German army, flushing out Marxists, and then he became an army educational officer, where he discovered and developed his oratorical powers. In September 1919, at age thirty, Hitler infiltrated a small Munich group called the German Workers' Party, and was so impressed with this tiny, disorganized, nationalistic, pro-military, anti-Semitic organization that he was persuaded to join.

Hitler soon became its star speaker, and also took charge of propaganda. He introduced the swastika as the party's symbol, and the party swelled its ranks, thanks largely to Hitler's rowdy polemical speeches. The founding members considered Hitler too extreme, but he blackmailed them into making him leader by threatening to leave. Rather than lose their angry golden boy, on July 29, 1921, all but one party member voted him Führer of the newly-renamed National Socialist German Workers' Party, better known as the Nazi Party.

WHY DO FLAMINGOS STAND ON ONE LEG?

The flamingo's one-legged stance always captures the public's imagination. A flamingo can stand on one leg for up to four hours and even sleep in that position. What leads this magnificent bird to behave in such a curious way?

The reason is a bit of a mystery, but biologists have offered several explanations that range from foot drying to heat conservation.

The first benefit of keeping one foot out of the water for a prolonged period is that it can dry out. Imagine if you spent all your time standing in the bath. Within a few hours your feet would be soft and wrinkled. The flamingo has the same problem, so it alternates feet.

Flamingos need to find food, and some observers believe they have more success when standing on one leg because it makes them look like a tree rather than a big pink predator. Given that their main diet is algae and small crustaceans, this seems an unlikely explanation for their posture. Flamingos stick their heads in the water upside down, and then suck mud and water into the front of their beaks where it is filtered to remove the edible life forms. Also, they stand on two legs when they feed.

Another explanation is that flamingos keep half of their brains awake while the other half sleeps (this is how dolphins and ducks sleep), with the supporting leg controlled by the waking side of the brain. The tucked-up leg doesn't flop down because the ankle is high up on the leg, about where you'd expect the knee to be, and it has an ingenious locking mechanism so that the bird can snap its leg into position.

Possibly the most important reason flamingos keep one foot out of the water, tucked close into their body, is to conserve heat. Their legs are very long and have a large surface area which means that flamingos lose a lot of body heat through them. It takes a lot of energy to pump blood to a fully extended leg, which also puts strain on the heart. Remove one leg and the heart has an easier job. This would explain why flamingos stand on one leg in both cold and hot weather.

WHY DO I SEE STARS SOMETIMES WHEN I SNEEZE?

Sneezing creates pressure in your chest and head, including the eyeballs, which compresses the optic nerve and the retina (the area of light-sensitive cells at the back of the eye). They respond by turning the stimulus into patterns of light that look like stars. There's even a scientific name for them: "phosphenes," from the Greek words *phos* (light) and *phainein* (to show), which create the experience of seeing light without light entering the eye.

As a child you probably created phosphenes by closing your eyes and then gently pressing the lids against your eyeballs until you saw a kaleidoscope of ever-changing colors and patterns. The pressure stimulates the retina and the optic nerve, and it responds the only way it knows how, by turning the signals into light.

The same stars will appear if you get up too suddenly after bending down or if you bang your head. If you suffer from migraine headaches, you may be painfully familiar with them. People also report seeing phosphenes after a long period without visual stimulation (earning it the nickname "prisoner's cinema").

Another curious visual anomaly, similar to phosphenes, are "floaters," which appear as specks floating across the field of vision, especially when individuals stare at a uniform background, such as a blue sky. These are caused by stray blood cells or turbulence inside the eyeball (which is filled with gel). Floaters are more common in older people, as the gel becomes thinner.

Phosphenes can be induced by electrical and magnetic stimulation, as well as a sneeze or a poke in the eye. Electrical stimulation of the visual cortex has been used to create rudimentary light patterns, such as Braille spots, so they have practical scientific applications as well as providing harmless entertainment for generations of bored and inquisitive children.

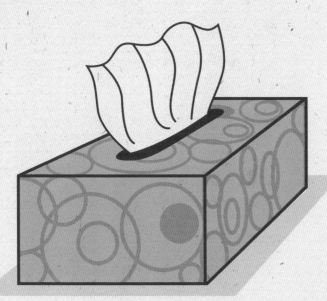

HOW CAN I OPEN A SWISS BANK ACCOUNT?

There are two main types of Swiss bank account: the notorious numbered private Swiss bank account and the regular Swiss bank account. Unless you have at least $300,000 to deposit, and the right connections, you can forget about a numbered account.

Swiss bankers are the most prestigious in the world, and the nation's economy is one of the most stable. With the exclusive numbered bank account, all transactions refer only to the number of the account. Knowledge of who owns the account is limited to a select few senior bankers. But it's still well worth getting a regular Swiss bank account, because Swiss banks have some of the tightest regulations in the world. It's a crime for a banker to disclose any information about a bank account, or even that it exists.

If someone suspects you're a crook and you have deposited money in an account, the burden of proof lies with them to convince a judge that you have committed a crime and that the account exists. Even if you are being investigated for tax evasion, the Swiss bank will not hand over your banking details, because failure to report income or assets is not a crime in Switzerland. Similar protection is offered to those going through a divorce: unless the plaintiff can prove that a bank account exists, they can't get at the money.

Opening an account is easy. You can do it in person, by post, or online. If you open the account in person you will need to make an appointment, and then bring proof of citizenship and country of residence, proof of address, and several other forms of identification. The account is opened the same day. Minimum deposits vary but usually start at around $200.

If you open the account by mail or the Internet you must first send an application; if this is approved you pay a set-up fee and the bank mails you documents which you must date, sign, and return along with other documents proving your identity, your address, and where the money came from. The whole process should take about ten days.

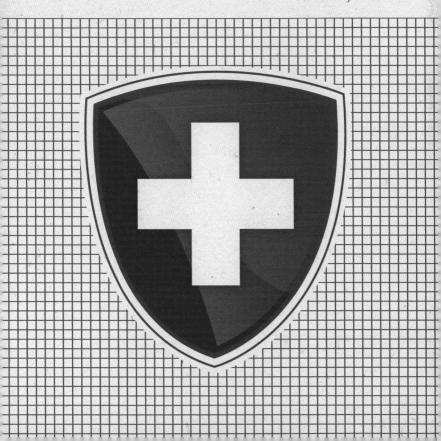

WHY DO MEN FALL ASLEEP AFTER SEX?

It is a familiar complaint of women that immediately after sex, no matter how passionate the encounter, men tend to roll over, nod off, and even start snoring. Their partners are left wide-awake, feeling abandoned. So what is it that makes men so sleepy after the act? Is it biological, or are they all a bunch of insensitive boors?

The first factor that is obvious, but needs pointing out, is that sex often happens at night and in bed, and can be quite physically exhausting. It shouldn't be surprising, therefore, that all the post-coital visual and physical cues are telling the man to grab some shuteye.

Secondly, many people hold their breath before and during orgasm, and when this follows a period of hyperventilating, drowsiness is inevitable because of the decreased oxygen exchange in the body: the body shuts down so the brain can replenish its oxygen supply. However, that should affect men and women equally, so what else is going on?

When a man orgasms, his brain releases a veritable pharmacy of brain- and mood-altering chemicals including norepinephrine, serotonin, oxytocin, vasopressin, nitric oxide, and prolactin. There is a strong link between prolactin and sleep: animals injected with it fall rapidly asleep. Oxytocin and vasopressin relax and de-stress the body, making sleep more compelling. More interesting though is the other effect of these last two chemicals: they facilitate pair bonding. From an evolutionary perspective, then, they create a stronger unit for breeding and raising young. Oxytocin is also found in breast milk, and helps suckling babies to sleep after feeding.

CAN ANIMALS SMELL FEAR?

No one can "smell" fear because it is an emotion, not a smell. So the real question is, "Can animals smell the chemicals released by other animals when they are frightened?" Many animals release stress pheromones when they sense danger, and members of the same species can pick these up. However, there is little evidence to demonstrate that this ability works between species. Animals don't rely on smell alone; they also observe and react to visual, aural, and behavioral clues, so their perception of fear and danger is multi-sensory.

Novice horse riders may well be advised not to let the horse smell their fear, but in fact the horse would pick up on a variety of non-olfactory cues such as hesitancy, overenthusiastic use of the reins, kicking too much, and other erratic behavior caused by uncertainty and apprehension. A dog can easily recognize that a human backing away while keeping unnaturally stiff is not showing normal human behavior.

Mice can smell the chemicals released by the other mice when they are frightened. In 1973, Swiss researchers discovered and named an organ called the Grueneberg ganglion at the end of mice snouts (humans also have one), which produces stress pheromones. They showed that mice are able to detect the alarm pheromones of dying mice (poisoned by carbon dioxide). Mice that had the ganglion surgically removed could detect hidden cookies but no longer responded fearfully to the alarm pheromones.

The stress response in humans is expressed in a number of ways: an increase in heart rate, release of glucose into the bloodstream, pupil dilation, elevated breathing, increased sweating, and in extreme situations, erratic movements and screaming. Any one of these responses could be detected by other animals.

Humans have two types of sweat glands: eccrine glands, which regulate body temperature, and apocrine glands (found in greatest concentration in the armpits and groin), which respond to stress and sexual stimulation. When a person is frightened or sexually aroused, these glands intensify the body odor, which other animals will be able to smell. If those animals are predators (e.g., a hungry lion) then this body odor would send an even more powerful signal to the animal that prey was available. Body odor alone, however, does not necessarily signal stress or danger to animals of a different species.

Grueneberg ganglion

WHY DO WE ALWAYS SEE THE SAME "FACE" ON THE MOON?

We only see one side of the moon from Earth for the simple reason that the rotation of the moon and the Earth are synchronized. The moon makes one rotation every 29 days, 12 hours, 44 minutes, and 3 seconds (on average), and that's the same time it takes for the moon to make one complete revolution around the Earth. This wasn't always so—a long time ago the moon and Earth were out of synch, but over millions of years, Earth's gravity has slowed down the moon's rotation.

This doesn't mean that we only see 50 percent of the moon. The moon is a sphere, so we only see 41 percent of it at any one time. But we do see more than that in total over time. The moon turns on its axis at a constant speed, but at some points on its orbit around Earth it will travel faster, because the moon follows an elliptical (rather than circular) orbit around the Earth. This makes the moon appear to wobble from side to side, revealing a total of 59 percent of its surface over time to anyone watching from Earth.

These irregular motions of the moon are called "librations" and they occur both latitudinally and longitudinally. There are also diurnal (daily) librations which occur when the moon is rising and setting. We can see a little more of the bottom of the moon when it is setting and a little more of the top when it is rising because the radius of the Earth adds an extra 4,000 miles of height to our vantage point when the moon is on the horizon.

The side of the moon we never see is referred to as the "Dark Side of the Moon," a misleading name since it suggests that one side of the moon is in permanent darkness. In fact, there is day and night on the moon as it rotates on its axis, although days and nights on the moon are nearly fifteen times longer than they are on Earth.

WHY DO WE HAVE AN APPENDIX?

Every year in the United States about 300,000 people have their appendix removed and live quite happily without it. So what, if anything, does it do, and why don't we need it?

A normal appendix is a tiny finger-shaped tube between three to four inches long, attached to the cecum, or first part of the large intestine. For many years it was widely considered to be a vestigial organ that served a function in our evolutionary past but that is now redundant. Some biologists believe it may have played a role in the digestive system when ancient humans ate more roughage. But few other mammals have an appendix, and there is little evidence to support the idea that our evolutionary ancestors did.

Recent studies have shown that the appendix has a high concentration of infection-fighting lymphoid cells, which means that it may play a role in boosting the immune system by helping a type of white blood cell mature as well as producing certain antibodies. Also, in the womb, the appendix of fetuses produces compounds that help to regulate various body functions.

A novel hypothesis published in *The Journal of Theoretical Biology* in December 2007 suggests that the appendix is where commensal bacteria (the "good" germs that aid digestion) hide out during times of crisis, thus avoiding pathogens in the rest of the gut. Once the infection has been flushed out (e.g., by a bout of diarrhea—a common bodily response to infection), the good germs can come out of hiding and re-colonize the intestine. If that were the case, it would mean that removing the appendix would compromise the immune system. But since outbreaks of intestinal disease are less common today than they were in times past, there is little chance of the commensal bacteria being wiped out completely. So if your appendix becomes inflamed, don't dwell on its possible benefits—get to hospital immediately because untreated appendicitis can be fatal.

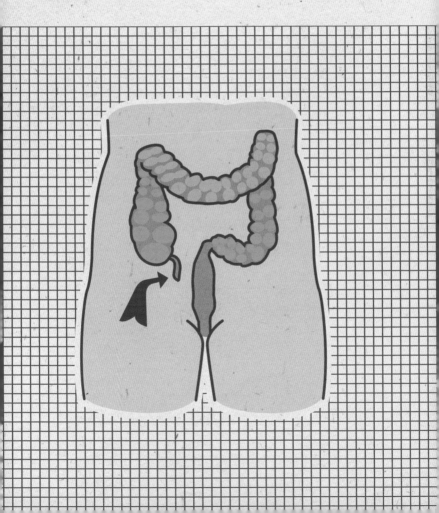

WHY DO WE NEED TO SLEEP?

We spend about one-third of our lives sleeping—but why? Most scientists agree that sleep is an anabolic, or building process, during which the body repairs itself, muscles rest, and important chemicals such as growth hormone are released. Children need growth hormone to grow, but adults also need it to repair the body. Sleeping does not conserve a significant amount of energy as such because it still takes a lot of energy to keep the metabolism functioning. The energy saved during sleep is about 50 kilocalories, equivalent to the energy expended eating a small apple.

The only animal that doesn't sleep is the bullfrog. Some animals, such as dolphins, allow half of their brain to sleep while the other half stays awake to regulate their breathing. But humans, like most animals, need to sleep; it is necessary for survival.

Clearly the body needs sleep in order to repair itself, but the organ that suffers the most from lack of sleep is the brain. We often think of sleep as a time of brain rest, but in fact brain activity doesn't slow down when we sleep, it just occurs in different areas and performs different functions, such as storing and sifting information. Studies have shown that after just seventeen hours of being awake, the brain experiences a reduction in function equivalent to that caused by drinking two glasses of wine. Prolonged sleep deprivation causes grumpiness, diminished ability to think and make rational judgments, reduction in physical coordination, irritability, forgetfulness, and even hallucinations.

Lack of sleep has also been shown to lead to obesity, since it increases the production of ghrelin, a hormone that increases the craving for food, and decreases leptin, a hormone that suppresses appetite.

The most famous case of sleep deprivation is that of Randy Garner, a San Diego high-school student who chose to stay awake for 264 hours (11 days) from December 28, 1963 to January 8, 1964. As the days passed, he suffered serious cognitive and behavioral changes. His speech became increasingly slurred, his short-term memory was severely diminished, and he experienced frequent dizziness and paranoia. At one stage the skinny seventeen-year-old white kid believed that he was Paul Lowe, a large black running back for the San Diego Chargers. At a press conference on the eleventh day he declared, "I wanted to prove that bad things didn't happen if you went without sleep." After his marathon ordeal, he slept for 14 hours and 45 minutes, woke feeling refreshed and alert, and then stayed up for another 24 hours.

HOW MUCH WOULD THE $15 MILLION PAID FOR THE LOUISIANA PURCHASE BE WORTH TODAY?

In 1803 the French, who three years earlier had only just acquired the territory of Louisiana through a secret treaty with the Spanish, agreed to sell it to the United States of America for $11,250,000. In addition the United States agreed to cancel $3,750,000 of French debt. The Americans made a down payment of $3 million in gold and borrowed the rest of the money from Dutch and British banks at a rate of 6 percent interest, which they repaid over twenty years. The total cost, including interest and the debt write-off, came to $23,213,568. This equals approximately $465 million in today's money. Clearly Napoleon sold these 828,800 square miles of land for a song, as it equates to four cents an acre in old money and eighty cents an acre today.

The French sold the territory cheaply because Napoleon was forced to abandon his plans for an empire in the New World after a large French force was defeated in the Caribbean. Initially, Thomas Jefferson sent James Monroe and Robert R. Livingstone to Paris to negotiate the purchase of New Orleans, in order to safeguard America's "right of deposit" and the right to navigate the Mississippi, which was essential for transportation and trade. He authorized them to pay a maximum of $10 million. However, Napoleon offered to sell the whole of Louisiana for $15 million. Unable to contact Jefferson for permission, they agreed. After the signing, Livingstone made the famous statement, "We have lived long but this is the noblest work of our whole lives . . . The United States take rank this day among the first powers of the Earth."

Jefferson had to set aside his principles in order to allow the sale to come before Congress. He didn't believe that the Constitution gave him the authority to acquire land. Furthermore, he believed that doing so would increase federal executive power to the detriment of individual states. This was too good an offer, however, to refuse for the sake of a principle. The land was eventually divided to make part of thirteen current states and two Canadian provinces.

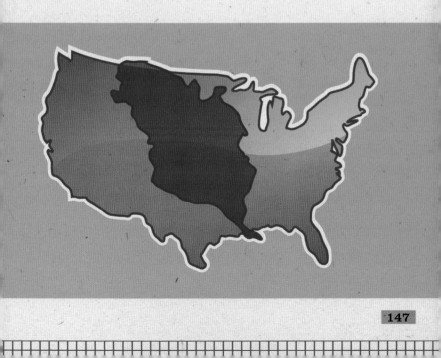

WHY DO MEN HAVE NIPPLES?

All men used to be women—in the womb. That's why they have nipples, which develop during the third or fourth week of gestation.

All human embryos begin life as females. If the embryo has a Y chromosome it will develop into a male; the female sex organs grow into a penis and testicles, but the nipples remain. Mind you, male nipples aren't merely vestigial. They and the chest area are still supplied by the requisite blood vessels and nerves to enable them to develop into breasts in the presence of large quantities of the female hormone estrogen, as happens when male transsexuals have corrective drug treatment, or when men develop gynecomastia (breast enlargement) due to a hormone imbalance. In certain circumstances these breasts can even lactate.

Some argue that Darwinian selection dictates that redundant body parts should disappear, in which case nipples should have a function in men. Not so. Evolution is littered with the remnants of what we used to be. In the womb we also sport a fine set of rudimentary gills and a tail. The gills disappear and the tail turns into the coccyx, or tailbone. Male nipples haven't disappeared yet, but unless another use can be found for them, they probably will eventually.

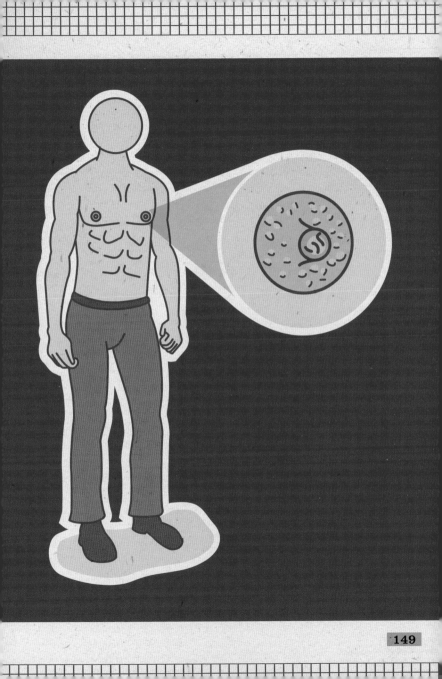

CAN I DIE OF A BROKEN HEART?

Indeed, you can. Doctors have discovered that people who are otherwise healthy and who have no risk indicators for heart attack such as high blood pressure, cholesterol, or blocked arteries can still suffer a condition called "stress cardiomyopathy," also known as "broken heart syndrome." It occurs after a sudden trauma including a breakup or the death of a loved one. Women—especially older women—are more susceptible than men.

People who are admitted to the hospital with a broken heart exhibit the same shortness of breath and tightness in the chest experienced by a typical heart-attack sufferer, but the cause is very different. In the case of a broken heart, extreme stress can trigger the release of dangerously high levels of catecholamines (including adrenalin and noradrenalin) which can stun the heart, causing it to malfunction. If treated, patients can make a full recovery within a few days, with no lasting heart damage, unlike heart attack patients who often take months to recuperate.

Echocardiogram data has shown that broken heart syndrome weakens contractions in the middle and upper part of the heart, while the base of the heart remains unaffected. It also shows up as a distinctive pattern on an electrocardiogram. Cardiologist Hunter Champion from John Hopkins School of Medicine admits that the way stress hormones stun the heart isn't fully understood, but he offers several possibilities: "The chemicals may cause spasm in the coronary arteries, or have a direct toxic effect on the heart muscle, or cause calcium overload that results in temporary dysfunction."

The negative effect on health of powerful emotions such as grief is still severely underestimated in the medical profession, despite the fact that a 2004 study published in the *Lancet* showed that stress and other psychological factors were more significant indicators of heart attack risk than family history.

Top U.S. cardiologist Dr. Mimi Guarneri is leading the charge for a more holistic approach to cardiac care: "We feel with our hearts, we love with our hearts, we can die of a broken heart. The most difficult job for a cardiologist is not picking the right medication but instilling in someone a passion for their life."

WHY IS FRIDAY THE 13TH CONSIDERED UNLUCKY?

Friday is named for the Norse female deity Freya, goddess of sex and fertility, who was associated with cats and worshipped on the sixth day. In Roman mythology she corresponded to Venus, the goddess of Love, who was also worshipped on the sixth day. Therefore, in pre-Christian cultures Friday was a good day for matters of the heart, such as getting married. As with many pagan customs and beliefs, though, Friday got a bad rap from Christians, and became a sort of pagan anti-Sabbath. Freya was transformed into a witch to be feared and reviled along with her sacred animal, the cat.

There are lots of inauspicious Fridays in Christian religious tradition. Friday is the day that Jesus was crucified, Adam and Eve ate the forbidden fruit, the Temple of Solomon was destroyed, the Great Flood started, and the builders of the Tower of Babel were struck dumb.

It has been suggested that suspicion of the number thirteen dates as far back as the time of primitive humans whom, according to theory, could only count using ten fingers and two feet, and treated any number greater than twelve with mistrust. On the other hand many pre-Christian cultures, such as the Chinese and the Ancient Egyptians, considered thirteen to be lucky. Others suggest that thirteen went out of favor when patriarchal religions and the solar calendar with its twelve months took over from matriarchal moon-worshipping cultures for whom thirteen corresponded to the number of lunar cycles and female menses in a year. Having thirteen guests at a meal is considered unlucky in many cultures. In Viking mythology Loki, the Evil One, crashed a banquet attended by twelve gods of Valhalla and caused the death of Balder. There were thirteen people at the last supper, one of whom betrayed Jesus, and the Hindus still avoid inviting thirteen guests to a gathering.

It remains a mystery why and how Friday and the number thirteen came together to create double jeopardy three times each year. One possible explanation is that King Philip IV of France began his routing of the Knights Templar on October 13, 1307—a Friday. However, there is no documented evidence that people considered Friday the 13th unlucky prior to the nineteenth century, so all the examples above may be revisionist history.

CAN I SAVE MYSELF FROM AN ELEVATOR CRASH BY JUMPING OFF AT THE MOMENT OF IMPACT?

It depends on the speed of the elevator and how high you can jump. If the elevator was going fairly slowly at, say, 10 mph, then of course jumping off wouldn't do much harm, but then neither would staying put. But in the case of a broken cable scenario with the elevator hurtling towards the ground at 100 mph, it's probably worth having a go.

If you were traveling on a train at 70 mph and you sprinted backwards at a speed of 25 mph and jumped off the back of the train, you would continue to travel forwards at a speed of 45 mph (70 minus 25). It's the same with the elevator. Unless you can jump upwards at something like 80 mph (which means jumping about 200 feet into the air), you aren't going to be able to compensate enough for your downward momentum to prevent serious injury or death.

The world record for height of a jump from a standing start is about 3 feet, which corresponds to a vertical velocity of about 9.5 mph, with an acceleration of approximately 10 ft/sec^2; if timed precisely at the moment of impact, this would result in you shaving 30 mph off the speed of the impact. If the elevator was traveling any faster than 60 mph, though, you'd still be in big trouble.

You'd also have to know exactly when to jump. If you happened to be traveling in a glass-bottomed elevator, you could see the ground approaching and time it correctly. All things considered, it's probably worth a try jumping upward. If luck is on your side you'll time it perfectly, and the adrenaline generated by the crisis will give you the sort of power that enables people to lift cars off their loved ones, and maybe to save your life. You'll jump higher and faster than Michael Jordan ever did.

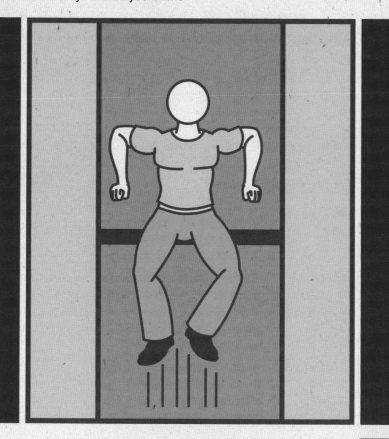

HOW DO WHALES HAVE SEX?

The sexual activity of whales is a fascinating topic, and it differs considerably between species. Killer whales can be sexually differentiated by the shape of their dorsal fins, but the sex of all other whale species can only be determined by examining the genital slit. In females it is at the base of the belly, while the male's is halfway between the anus and the base of the belly. The penis and testicles hide inside the slit, which keeps them warm and protected and allows for maximum aerodynamics.

As you would expect, there is intense competition between males, which sometimes involves physical combat or leaping out of the water in elaborate displays of agility and strength. Some whale species compete mainly in terms of the quantity of sperm they can produce. The female has sex with several partners, so the more sperm the male can produce, the greater his chances of making the female pregnant. Consequently some species have very heavy testicles in relation to their body weight. The right whale has the biggest testicles, weighing more than 1,000 pounds and accounting for 1 percent of its body weight.

There haven't been many sighting of whales having sex in the wild. It mostly occurs underwater, either belly-to-belly or sideways. Mating often involves energetic high-speed chases, tail slapping, and breaching. Sometimes a pair will rise out of the water tail first, belly-to-belly, and hold this position for several seconds. Whales have a repertoire of clicks and elaborate hunting songs that the female uses to judge the size of her potential mates in order to find the biggest. The lower the call the bigger the whale.

HOW LONG CAN I LIVE WITHOUT FOOD OR WATER?

The human body can survive for weeks without food. Water is a different story. A person will die within 3 to 4 days without water. The size of the person really doesn't make much difference.

Water constitutes the basic milieu in which chemical reactions occur in every organ of the body. Your brain, which enables you to read this book, is about 75 percent water. Your body is 70 percent water. Water helps to regulate body temperature, carries energy, and helps to expel waste. Since most of the important reactions that sustain life occur in body cells, it is not surprising that at least 35 percent of our lean body weight (LBW) consists of water within cells. Our total blood volume accounts for only 5 percent of LBW.

Each day of our life sees an exchange of water taking place in our bodies. Our lungs exhale approximately one-third of a liter of water daily and our skin sweats away about one-half liter through the 2 million sweat glands in our skin. In addition, we excrete approximately one-and-a-half liters of water per day.

Water is essential to maintain the important balance within our system. If what goes out and what goes in do not come within 1 to 2 percent of each other, we experience either thirst or pain. If the body loses 5 percent of its total water, hallucinations will result. A loss of 15 percent is usually fatal.

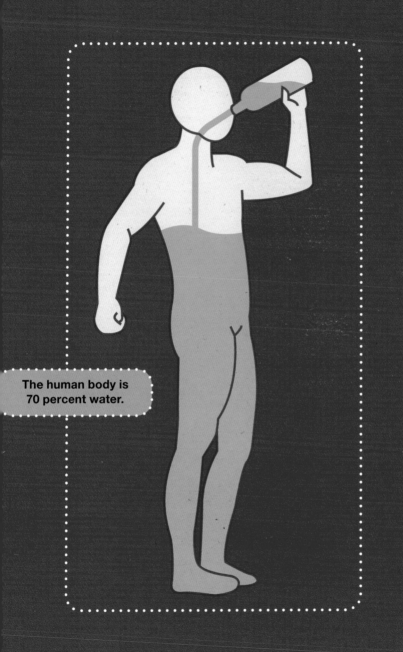

The human body is
70 percent water.

A person can live

without food for

quite some time,

usually for many weeks.

A person can live without food for quite some time, usually for many weeks. The body will use its fat and protein stores (muscles) to help it survive. A person with a lot of fat stores will live longer than a person who has very little fat. How long a person can survive on water alone, therefore, depends a lot on the person. Of course, if you go without food for a few weeks, you will be very weak since you will have converted your own muscles into energy.

In conclusion, if you were on a desert island and someone offered you a bathtub full of water or a table full of food, you should definitely go for the water.